MORE PRAISE FOR KOSHER JESUS

"It is tragic that two great religions that worship the same God, cherish the same Scriptures and affirm the same moral code have been so antagonistic to each other for so long. May this book help to heal that breach."

Rabbi Harold Kushner,
Author of When Bad Things Happen To Good People

———

"In Kosher Jesus, Rabbi Shmuley explores the complicated and controversial relationship between Jesus, the Jews and the Christians. In this provocative and thought provoking book, Shmuley tackles the issues with intelligence and compassion and offers new insights which provide a bridge to greater understanding for people of all faiths."

Lisa Oz,
Author and Radio Host

———

"Rabbi Shmuley offers a fascinating view of Jesus through the eyes of an orthodox Rabbi. Every time a Jewish friend examines the life of Jesus, it makes me wish I had grown-up Jewish. While I don't agree with his every conclusion, it is a fascinating read. I am grateful he has given me a view of his journey."

V. Glen Megill,
Founder & President ROCK of Africa Mission,
a Christian outreach to Africa

———

"Rabbi Shmuley is a man from a strict orthodox background who offers a unique examination of Jesus, the man. Few evangelical Christians can really understand how difficult it is to do what Rabbi Shmuley has done. I pray his journey will continue."

Dr. Kenton Beshore,
Founder & President World Bible Society

"**W**hile finding myself in profound disagreement with point after point in this book, most particularly Shmuley's reconstruction of the New Testament and his passionate rejection of Jesus as our Messiah, I am thrilled to see an Orthodox Rabbi embracing Jesus as a fellow Rabbi, not to mention as an important figure in Jewish history. In fact, this book might be described as, "America's most famous Rabbi meets the most famous Rabbi of all time."

Dr. Michael Brown,
President of Fire School of Ministry and author,
Answering Jewish Objections to Jesus

———

"**R**abbi Shmuley explores and logically explains, many of the historical and religious writings, which have been responsible for the 2000-year-old schism between Jews and Christians. I disagree however completely with his assessment of Pope Pius XII, which new research is beginning to show offers a much altered view of what Rabbi Shmuley conveys in his book."

Gary L. Krupp,
President and Founder of Pave The Way Foundation

———

"**S**hmuley Boteach is among the most provocative and creative minds involved in public discourse. Once again, he tackles a fascinating and controversial topic, shedding light and bringing insight to a subject many have shied away from."

Gregory Zuckerman,
Author of "The Greatest Trade Ever"

KOSHER JESUS

RABBI SHMULEY BOTEACH

kosher
JESUS

Cover Design: Budi Setiawan
Typesetting: David Yehoshua

ISBN: 978-965-229-578-1

3 5 7 9 8 6 4 2

Gefen Publishing House Ltd.
6 Hatzvi Street
Jerusalem 94386, Israel
972-2-538-0247
orders@gefenpublishing.com

Gefen Books
11 Edison Place
Springfield, NJ 07081, USA
516-593-1234
orders@gefenpublishing.com

This World: The Values Network
PO Box 61
Englewood, NJ 07631
www.thisworld.us
www.shmuley.com

www.gefenpublishing.com

Printed in Israel

Send for our free catalogue

Library of Congress Cataloging-in-Publication Data

Boteach, Shmuel.
    Kosher Jesus / Shmuley Boteach.
      p. cm.
    Includes bibliographical references.
    ISBN 978-965-229-578-1
    1. Jesus Christ–Jewish interpretations. 2. Judaism–Relations–Christianity.
    3. Judaism–Relations–Christianity. I. Title.
BM620.B68 2011
296.3'96–dc23
                                         2011035274

To my daughter
my eldest child
Chaya Mushka (Mushki)

and her bridegroom
Arye Zev (Arik)

on the occasion of their marriage

I am thrilled to see you as a *kallah* (bride), Baby Girl.
May G-d grant you both love and joy,
peace and blessing,
spiritual light and material plenty.

… And may He walk with you always.

CONTENTS

Part V

RESTORING JUDEO-CHRISTIAN VALUES

PREFACE

This book tells what I believe to be the true story of Jesus of Nazareth.

Growing up in an Orthodox Jewish household, I held great antipathy toward Jesus. The very name reminded me of the suffering Christians laid upon Jewish communities for two thousand years: persecutions, forced conversions, expulsions, inquisitions, false accusations, degradations, economic exile, taxation, pogroms, stereotyping, ghettoization, and systematic extermination. All this incomprehensible violence and cruelty against us – against our friends and families – committed in the name of a Jew!

In my neighborhood, we did not even mention his name. We said "Yoshke," a Hebrew play on his name, or some children learned to say "cheese and crust" in place of "Jesus Christ." In a synagogue sermon, rabbis might refer to Jesus – exceedingly rarely – by saying "the founder of Christianity."

Fundamentally, we understood Jesus as a foreign deity, a man worshipped by people. The Torah instructs us never to mention the names of other gods, as no other god exists except God. We also understood Jesus to be as anti-Jewish as his followers. Was he not the Jew who had rebelled against his people? Was he not the one who instructed his followers to hate the Jews as he did, instigating countless cruelties against those with whom God had established an everlasting covenant? Was he not also the man who had abrogated the Law and said that the Torah is now mostly abolished?

In truth, Jesus was not that man. The more I studied the matter, the more I discovered Jesus had done none of these things. The people who represented him in this way had a vested interest in doing so. They superimposed onto Jesus their own antipathy toward Jews. They ripped a Jewish patriot away from his people. They portrayed his teachings as being hostile to Judaism when, in fact, everything he taught stemmed from the Judaism he practiced.

I seek to correct this injustice at long last. Just as Christians would greatly benefit from a deeper understanding of Jesus the man, Jews need to accept that they have something to learn from Jesus as well, albeit in a manner very different from the way that Christians understand him. Nearly all his authentic lessons were restatements of classical Torah wisdom, and his ethical teachings still have the power to speak to us today. Awareness of their truths would enrich a Jewish community that, by rejecting the fictional, anti-Semitic Jesus, has mistakenly rejected the man himself.

In these pages, based on ancient Hebrew sources as well as Christian scripture, you will discover the authentic story of Jesus of Nazareth.

Jesus lived, taught, and died as a Jew. He defined himself and his Jewishness in much the same way as today's Torah-observant Jews. He conducted himself as a devout rabbi and Pharisee. He wore a Jewish head covering, prayed in the Hebrew language, ate only kosher food, honored the Sabbath, had the mezuzah parchment on the doorposts of his home, lit a Chanukah menorah, wore the tzitzit-fringes, donned tefillin daily, waved an *esrog* and *lulav* on Sukkot, ate matzo on Passover, and studied the Torah regularly. He enjoyed the selfsame relationship with God shared by all Jews.

Though this book does not consider Jesus holier than any other human being and certainly not divine, I argue that Jews *should* claim him as one of our own. Through Jewish sensibilities, we can see in the Christian Bible one of our rabbis, Jesus, ever our brother. As Jews, we should celebrate the family bond we have with Jesus. We also have a bond with Christianity, even as our faiths differ considerably in many aspects. Ultimately, this book aims to initiate a wider celebration of both bonds and differences, for each delivers distinctive joy.

Introduction

Who Was Jesus of Nazareth?

The genesis of this book is a simple question: Who was Jesus of Nazareth?

We all *think* we know who he was – the inspiration for the world's most successful religion. The deliverer of faith, love, spiritual inspiration, and religious commitment to billions of people the world over for two millennia. Christians see him as the son of God, both wholly human and wholly divine, whose example, compassion, and self-sacrifice are a bulwark for the faithful worldwide.

But is that the whole story?

This question has dominated my twenty years of in-depth study of the New Testament and Christianity. The answers I have found have been sharpened by challenges, years of discussion, and debate (many available on YouTube and on my website) with leading Christian scholars all around the world. My opinions on Jesus have been profoundly shaped by the writings of Hyam Maccoby and his compelling insights into the historical Jesus. This book would not have been possible without Mr. Maccoby's work, which serves as a pivotal foundation and central pillar for what follows here. More than any other works of scholarship, Maccoby's books get to the very heart of the historical Jesus, and I am profoundly indebted to him for his lifelong research. His insights, more than anyone else's, have illuminated for me the real truth of the Jewish Jesus, and I strongly encourage the reader to dip directly into his texts, as even this book is an insufficient substitute.

For all the undeniable good Christianity has done, even its most passionate adherents would admit it has also been directly and indirectly responsible for a great deal of suffering. Until the modern era, Christian history is rife with physical violence and discrimination. Awful acts of hatred and intolerance were committed in Jesus' name. And for far too long, the received picture of Jesus has obscured a simple and powerful truth: Jesus would never stand as an enemy against his own people, nor would he tolerate his followers doing so.

From the very beginning, as Christianity branched away from Judaism to develop its own identity, Jesus was intentionally shorn of his Jewishness like Samson deprived of his strength. Christians obfuscated the idea of Jesus the Jew, preferring to see him as an innovator who at once transcended Judaism and brought it to a conclusion. This deception deeply alienated Jesus from the Jewish people and led to considerable torment and distress.

This is not to suggest that the chilly relationship between Christians and Jews was one-sided. Jews have long avoided any connection to Jesus. Over the centuries, as he was slowly turned into a deity and violence perpetrated in his name against the Jews increased, they came to see him as a source of unrelenting persecution, the supreme example of heresy. They wanted no association with the patron saint of zealots who demeaned, attacked, and murdered them, and taught sacrilege in his name.

But times are changing. Christianity has opened its heart to the Jews.

The Catholic Church is today a great friend to the Jewish people. In May 2010, as a guest of the Vatican, I met Pope Benedict; his warmth and regard for me as a rabbi were immediately in evidence. Evangelical Christians are among the most stalwart supporters of the State of Israel. Not only that, of the 3.45 million tourists who visited the Jewish homeland in 2010, 69 percent were Christians. I am personally in awe of the stalwart and unwavering support offered to the

State of Israel by evangelical Christians, and I have thanked them time and again in their churches and in op-eds.

Christians are beginning to take a long-overdue look back on the common origins of our religious outlook with modern eyes and see how we got to where we are.

Now, perhaps it's time and equally imperative that Jews recognize a long-obscured and essential truth: Rabbi Jesus was a Jew and should be counted among our nation. The heroic Jewish patriot you will encounter in these pages should not be severed from the people he loved and the people he died defending.

SUPPLANTING JUDAISM

Unlike many other religions that came into being independently, Christianity entered the world claiming to fulfill Judaic prophesy. Competition with Judaism was built into Christianity from its inception, priming early Christians to harbor immediate hostility toward Jews despite, or perhaps because of, their religious commonalities.

Some early Christian fathers felt the need to directly discredit Jews and Judaism. To them, the very idea of "righteous" Jews or "just" Judaism contradicted the Christian premise outright. *How could Jews be just*, they thought, *when they're practicing the wrong religion!* Replacement theology, the deeply anti-Semitic belief that God discarded the Jews when they rejected Jesus and replaced them instead with Christians, has prevailed throughout Christendom for generations.

Until the deeply anti-Semitic Augustine of Hippo (354–430 CE) directly addressed the subject centuries later, early Church leaders held that Judaism would never survive. Even the powerful Roman Empire couldn't resist the Christian juggernaut – eventually capitulating and adopting Christianity as state religion. It wasn't a stretch for Christians to surmise that all remaining Jews would eventually convert, wiping out the ancient religion. But against all odds, Judaism survived and flourished.

As the years went by and the Jews failed to disappear, Christians grew anxious for an explanation. St. Augustine of Hippo provided it. The third most important figure in Christian theology after Jesus and Paul, Augustine argued that the Jews were actually part of God's master plan. For their rejection of Jesus, the Jews were eternally cursed, their ongoing existence and failure to accept Jesus seen as a proof of his messiahship, instead of its refutation. The Jews were destined to live on, depressed and miserable symbols of God's displeasure and the final triumph of Christianity over Judaism.

Insulting as this view was, it was something of an improvement. Many of Augustine's predecessors had advocated policies of forced conversion. Resistance led to expulsion from the community and harrowing executions. Relatively speaking, Augustine's position somewhat benefited Judaism since, even as he denigrated Jews, he at least argued Christians should not slaughter them.

Long after the violence and viciousness of this period ceased, enmity seethed under the surface. Jesus became the primary vehicle of controversy and disagreement between religions. Jews refused to study him, his teachings tainted by his role as the wellspring of anti-Jewish activities and hatred. Conversely, Christians ignored Jesus' Jewishness because they saw Judaism as a despised and obsolete religion. Traces of these attitudes continue to hold sway, even into today's era of heightened awareness and reconciliation.

PROGRESS

Over the past few decades, the two faiths have become closer allies, and Jews and Christians increasingly see one another as spiritual kin. This new era of brotherhood was forged in the horrors of the past hundred years, and results from outreach by both the Catholic and Evangelical Christian communities.

Three courageous popes emerged in the latter half of the twentieth century and showed themselves to be heroic friends of the Jewish people: John XXIII, the greatest of all popes; John Paul II, a magnificent friend of the Jewish community and of all humanity; and Benedict XVI, the modern theological father of rapprochement with the Jews, who gets far too little credit for the enormous efforts at reconciliation he has made.

Pope John XXIII was responsible for calling the Second Vatican Council, which in the early 1960s changed the course of Christian doctrine. Just one of many forward-looking changes that resulted was the renunciation of the Jews as *deicides*, or killers of God, a theological relic of the vitriolic anti-Semitism that once haunted mainstream Christianity. John XXIII also had worked actively to save Jewish lives during the Holocaust. When he invited Jewish groups to the Vatican, he would dismount from his papal throne and say humbly to them, "I am your brother Joseph." This is an unparalleled demonstration of humility and greatness that beggars belief.

John Paul II was a leader of extraordinary humanity and humility in his own right. He will always be remembered for opening Christian hearts to Jews, continuing the work that John XXIII began, and changing the tenor of Jewish-Christian relations. John Paul was the first pope in history to visit a synagogue, in this case the beautiful one in Rome.

Benedict XVI has also proven himself a great friend of the Jewish people. While he's received his share of criticism for the Church's mishandling of the pedophile priest scandal, it must not be forgotten he did more as prefect of the Congregation for the Doctrine of the Faith to extend the Church's hand in friendship to other peoples and faiths than nearly anyone who preceded him. As of this writing, Benedict has visited three synagogues in the six years of his papacy.

Theologians did their part to warm relations as well. In the 1960s and '70s, Krister Stendahl, among others, initiated a sea change in Jewish-Christian friendship by reevaluating the mandate for Christians to convert Jews. Examining Paul's letters to the Romans, Stendahl found "an affirmation of a God-willed coexistence between Judaism and Christianity in which the missionary urge to convert Israel is held in check."[1] He argued the Church had ignored this fact, permitting the relationship between gentiles and Jews to become all too focused on conversion instead of cooperation. This was a thoroughgoing reversal of established Christian doctrine. As its ramifications percolated through seminaries, world events further advanced Christian respect for Judaism.

The 1967 Six-Day War between Israel and the massed forces of Egypt, Syria, and Jordan gave American Christians a bona fide opening to embrace the miraculous nature of the modern Jewish state. The conflict ended in a stunning Israeli victory, pushing American Evangelicals to reconsider their stance on the Jewish nation. Their conclusion? In 1980, as dyed-in-the-wool a Christian Evangelical as Jerry Falwell wrote in his book *Listen America*, "Israel still stands as shining testimonial to the faithfulness of God." Gone were discussions of conversion and exhortations to evangelize the Jews. Instead, Falwell spoke of Israel in the highest terms. "There is no way that the tiny nation of Israel could have stood against the Arabs in the miraculous six-day war had it not been for the intervention of God Almighty."[2]

In the years since, the American Evangelical community has proven the most stalwart and reliable friend of Israel in the United States. In spite of a flare-up of discordant ideas resulting from Mel Gibson's film *The Passion of the Christ*, a movie I excoriated for its historical revisionism and blatant anti-Semitism, Evangelicals remain engaged and devoted friends of Israel and the Jewish people.

Christianity has established itself as a strong and independent religion, both valuable to the world and capable of tremendous good. It no longer defines itself by its opposition to Judaism. For the most part, Christians no longer feel the same antipathy toward Jews that they had for centuries.

It is time to build on these overtures of peace and address the first and last sticking point in the relationship between Christians and Jews: their common claim on Jesus.

THE FUTURE OF JESUS AND THE JEWS

The stage has been set for us to see Jesus for who he truly was: a wise and learned rabbi who despised the Romans for their cruelty to his Israelite brethren, who fought the Romans courageously and was ultimately murdered for trying to throw off the Roman yoke of oppression. He was a man who worked to rekindle Jewish ritual observance of every aspect of the Torah and to counter the brutal Roman occupation of his people's land. He never wavered in this mission even when he realized the consequences would be fatal. So greatly did Jesus love his people, so deeply did he believe in his messianic mission to grant the Jews independence from Rome, that he was willing to suffer and die to end Roman dominion and renew Jewish sovereignty in ancient Israel.

Even as I highlight the overlooked Jewish character of Jesus, the fact remains that Jews will never accept his divinity. Nor should they. The belief that any man is God is an abomination to Judaism, a position that Jesus himself would maintain. But this is decidedly not the same as seeing Jesus for the Jewish hero he undoubtedly was.

For thousands of years, just as they rejected his divinity, Jews have rejected the messiahship of Jesus as well. This too will never change, given that he died without fulfilling the messianic prophecies. But Jesus doesn't need to be the messiah to be a champion of the Jewish people. All Jews can embrace Jesus as part of a grand tradition of heroic leaders who fought to free Israel from tyranny. Looked at from this angle, Jesus was a great, world-changing patriot for Judaism. We commit no heresy by acknowledging that Jesus died valiantly defending his people as he tried but ultimately failed to become the Jewish messiah and bring about permanent security and peace for his people.

Jews no longer feel the same distrust and hostility toward Christianity that they did in past centuries. Rather than enemies, Christians and Jews now face each other as friends, even brothers. Together they confront the implacable foe of Islamist terrorism that has set its sights on the West. Such a moment marks the perfect time for a new exploration of Jesus' authentic Jewish identity.

Once we strip his life story of its patina of paganism and the supernatural, Jews will see they need no longer reject the beautiful ethical teachings of Jesus, which find their source in Hebrew scripture and the teachings of the rabbis among whom he counted himself. These can easily be traced back to their original Jewish sources. As I will demonstrate, his eloquent statements, lessons, and parables align with traditional Jewish belief, even as Christians viewing these messages in their original may see them as a departure from the traditional Christianity they know so well.

Fundamentally, Jews have the duty to ask themselves: Do we really profit by shunning a Jewish patriot who fought and died for our freedom? Jesus certainly was one of the most famous Jews that ever lived. Should he be forever lost to his people?

Without a doubt, there is much baggage to overcome. After millennia spent rejecting Jesus as a foreign god, the Jewish community will inevitably find it difficult to embrace Jesus on any level, purely for the reason of Christianity's more offensively anti-Semitic teachings. But the elements of Jesus' life and doctrine the Jews find objectionable would have given pause to Jesus himself, throwing their authenticity into question.

A crucial element of this book is Jesus' innocence in the smears that were attributed to him after the fact. The apostle Paul is directly responsible for introducing these elements years after Jesus' death. Paul never met Jesus, and Jesus certainly never would have sanctioned Paul's actions and embellishments. Even so, Paul developed the ideas and approaches that led people to view Jesus as the founder and focus of a new religion – one defined by its opposition to Judaism.

It is unjust to hold Jesus accountable for the millennia of anti-Semitism perpetrated in his name. Jesus was long dead when Augustine ruled Christians should look upon Jews as an accursed people. Jesus never urged crusaders onward as they marched through Europe massacring Jews. Jesus did not light the fires of the auto-da-fés in Catholic Spain. Jesus did not push the Jews across the Spanish-Portuguese border in the expulsion of 1492. Jesus did not torch Jewish homes in pogroms encouraged by European Christian clerics. And what he certainly did not do was put the Zyklon-B gas into the crematoria of Auschwitz.

We should not blame Jesus for these assaults against his people, his nation, and his kin. Judging from his actions during his life, he surely would have fought these developments with all his strength and led an outright revolt against such oppression.

ENRICHING CHRISTIANITY WITH A HEAVY SPRINKLING OF JEWISH SPICE

Christianity, too, has much to gain from a rediscovery of the authentic Jewishness of Jesus. American culture is less in accordance with Christian theology than many would think. Bringing a bit more Jewish influence to bear would make a great deal of sense for American Christians.

By discovering the Jewish Jesus and the Jewish understanding behind the bedrock premises of Christianity, Christians' understanding of their own faith will be enriched and riddles will be resolved. Modern American and Judeo-Christian values will be strengthened to the benefit of both Jewish and Christian communities and our society as a whole.

Much of what I am about to present cuts against conventional wisdom. I expect controversy and criticism by scholars and lay readers alike. For this reason, everything I present has scriptural and historical underpinnings, making a case that I believe will be persuasive. But even if a reader disagrees with the substance of my arguments, a far more enlightened understanding of Jesus will have been revealed.

ℰ℈

If I may summarize:

1. *The transformation of Jesus from lover of Israel to sworn enemy of the Jewish people constitutes one of the greatest acts of character assassination in all of human history.* It yielded tragic results for Jesus, for Judaism, and for Christianity. For Jesus because he became, certainly in the eyes of the Jews, not a prince of peace but an anti-Semitic bigot. For Judaism because the religion and its people became unprotected objects of cultural disenfranchisement and persecution for two thousand years. And for Christianity because the true identity of its central figure became obscured by doctrine and fiat. With this transformation, the Christian faith lost its anchor in Jewish spirituality.

2. *Once we see Jesus outside the anti-Jewish textual additions of the Gospels' redactors, Jews can finally re-embrace him as a fallen patriot*

and beloved son. Once we understand that Christian ideas of Jesus as divine messiah emerged as a savvy adaptation following the destruction of the Second Temple, Jews can take inspiration from Jesus' often beautiful ethical teachings, and appreciate Jesus as a devoted Jewish son who became martyred while trying to lift the Roman yoke of oppression from his beloved people.

3. *Restoring Jesus to his authentic Jewish roots can allow a new era of Jewish-Christian rapprochement to begin.* Jews and Christians may not meet in religious belief. Our theologies are different and sometimes contradictory. But for the first time in two millennia, we can forge a deep bond of togetherness using Jesus of Nazareth as a bridge, even as we understand him in completely different ways.

☙

It's important to be utterly clear: I neither seek nor hope for any Christian to convert from Christianity. I deeply respect the Christian faith of my Christian brothers and sisters and seek to reinforce it, albeit by enlightening Christians as to the Jewish underpinnings of Christianity. Moreover, we Jews do not proselytize. We are instead passionate advocates that all should "honor their incarnation," finding God in the religious tradition that is theirs alone. But if we are to disagree, let us at least learn from our differences.

I believe we religious folk must do a better job of intellectually handling and responding to challenges. These arguments should maintain a peaceful, intellectual quality and ought never stray from their overriding purpose: asserting the equal dignity of all religious systems.

Theologically, Christians and Jews think differently about the nature of the world. This will not and should not change. Religions have so much to teach each other precisely because they're different. Yet, more than any other two religious faiths, Christianity and

Judaism contain the elements for a lasting fellowship. Their long history has seen acrimony and much Jewish blood, to be sure; but also, in recent times, beautiful moments of tolerance, friendship, cooperation, and mutual enrichment and support. We should strive to forge from these moments a permanent alliance between Christianity and Judaism – one that pivots on a great personality both faiths hold in common.

Before we can do this, we will need to finally retire the twin falsehoods that Jesus was an enemy of Judaism, and that the Jews killed the son of God. A new era in Jewish-Christian brotherhood awaits us if we can only reverse these historical untruths, embracing Jesus for who he truly was. It is time to tell the story anew.

The world today needs both a philosophy of peace and leaders of peace. I feel deeply that Christians and Jews can supply both in great measure – and together form the visible vanguard for real *tikkun olam*, healing of the world. Surprising as it may sound to Jews, one of the important keys to it all is Jesus.

I humbly submit to readers of all faiths this renewed view of Jesus of Nazareth, a Jewish and kosher Jesus.

PART I

THE RABBI

CHAPTER 1

THE RABBI AND THE STRANGER

Come back with me two thousand years.

Our scene is a tumultuous province of the Roman Empire called Judea. There, the Jews are struggling to break free from the cruel dominion of the Romans. To the north, the region of Galilee harbors the most passionately rebellious anti-Roman sentiment of all. Its inhabitants hold fast to deep religious beliefs.

The Judeans despise the Romans for their brutality. The Roman occupation, deeply pagan in nature, has decimated much Jewish ritual observance. In desperation, some Jews have adopted the beliefs and practices of their Roman overlords. But the uniqueness of monotheistic Jewish belief distinguishes the Jews from other conquered people in the empire. They systematically reject Roman pagan beliefs and steadfastly hold to the Law of Moses. As a result, many Jews openly show contempt for Roman rule. They are different and they will not compromise their uniqueness.

The Roman proconsul in charge of the region is the tyrannical and murderous Pontius Pilate. Violent to his bloody core, he thinks nothing of executing anyone who gets in his way. Mass murder is his stock in trade. In later years, his vicious methods will derail his career. He will be recalled to Rome for being excessively violent, a singular achievement in the pitiless world of Rome. But for now, his Roman masters embrace the utility of his ruthlessness.

The residents of Galilee desperately yearn to overthrow Roman rule. They have suffered under barbarous foreign occupation for

3

more than a century. They seek to reestablish Jewish sovereignty and independence, but their small rebel bands cannot compete with the military might of the empire.

They pine for their redeemer, the long-promised Jewish messiah. Foretold by the Hebrew prophets, he is to be a hero who mingles spiritual greatness with military prowess. With God as his reinforcement, this hero will drive out the haughty legions of Rome once and for all.

THE TEACHER

A teacher emerges from the gloom. Only about thirty years old, he is blessed with extraordinary charisma. With remarkable courage, he rises up and publicly decries the Romans. In speeches from hilltops and market squares all over the Galilee, he proclaims that the Jews must earn their redemption. He exhorts his people to mindfully practice God's law once again. His ethical teachings eloquently delineate the differences between the monstrous crimes of Rome versus the call to compassion of the Jewish God. He inspires the wary Jews to overcome their fears of Rome. He broadcasts his call to arms far and wide, building a passionate and devoted following.

The teacher's rhetorical style is eclectic, complementing homespun parables with fierce fighting words to inspire in his listeners a craving for rebellion. If the Jews reassert their true fidelity to God, he says, they will be victorious. All of Rome's legions cannot overcome the Rock of Israel. Had God not destroyed the chariots of Pharaoh? Had He not helped David defeat Goliath? Had He not slaughtered Sennacherib's legions in their thousands when they camped outside Jerusalem? He will do so again.

At the heart of the teacher's message is a single commandment: his followers must recommit themselves to the Torah's laws and values. If they love each other and embrace true unity, their enemies can never break them. He amasses a huge following as his message of Jewish spiritual renaissance and contempt for Rome takes root. The time of redemption is approaching.

THE MESSIAH

The teacher's reputation is growing. His eloquence has captured a spirit of populism and an enthusiasm for Jewish self-rule. His speeches increase in their urgency. He tells his followers that the moment of redemption is drawing ever nearer. He has become certain of what he only suspected before: it is his destiny to lead God's children from oppressive Roman rule.

Now a messianic light guides him. He has become convinced that he is the long-promised Jewish redeemer. His followers believe it, too. He has been sent to them by none other than God Himself. If he will lead his disciples to Jerusalem, they whisper to one another, God Himself will march with them and establish His Kingdom with the sword as mere catalyst, the spirit of God their true shield and moral force.

The rabbi has nothing to fear from the massive Roman political and military forces that will seek to destroy him as they have so many others. God's own grace will protect him and his followers. God, the Shield of Israel, will deflect Rome's arrows and spears.

Like waves of the sea churning to a crest, the time has arrived. Passover, the festival of redemption, begins at sundown. In the midst of the celebration, the excitement becomes palpable and the rabbi's followers are reminded of times past, when God's might lifted Israel from bondage. The Lord split the sea for the former Hebrew slaves. Now, He will tear asunder the mighty legions of Rome. Just as Samson killed thousands of Philistines with the jawbone of an ass, the rabbi will beat back Rome's armies with his outstretched sword. Freedom is coming: they are sure of it.

The teacher travels with his disciples from Galilee to Jerusalem, the cradle of ancient Jewish civilization, currently besieged and contaminated by pagan Roman culture. Immense crowds of fellow Jews greet him and hail him as their leader. Yet he is not the first to receive such treatment. Many would-be messiahs have preceded him. They, too, claimed to be the promised Jewish redeemer and hurled themselves against Rome. All fell.

But something feels different this time. The rabbi exudes a sublime light. He swells with certainty, courage, and rhetorical brilliance. He uses accessible parables to communicate his deeply spiritual teachings. He inspires both the learned and the ignorant. The crowd recognizes him for what he is. He *must* be the one. Even the Roman emperor himself has not the power to stop the foretold messiah.

On the night before the final confrontation, the rabbi gathers his disciples together. He orders them to collect swords. They must prepare to seize the Temple by force. They will demonstrate to the people of Jerusalem their teacher's courage and fearlessness in the face of Rome. When the people see, they will follow him, sparking a massive rebellion. The Romans will have no choice but to retreat.

But he relies not on the sword alone. If he but makes the effort to begin the fight, God will take over and rescue His people. Just as the Israelites in their flight from Egypt needed to demonstrate faith by plunging into the churning waters, after which God parted the Red Sea, likewise the teacher and his disciples need only demonstrate sincere willingness to take on the enemy. Then, God will do the rest.

The Book of Deuteronomy declares, "The Lord will bless you in all that you endeavor." You must first endeavor, and God will then do His share. Moses defeated the Amalekites by raising his hands heavenward in a show of defiant faith. God rewards such trust even in the absence of numbers. The teacher holds every confidence that God will grant him a miracle as He did the Maccabees. That poorly equipped fighting force defeated the Assyrian Greeks two hundred years earlier in what became the miracle of Chanukah. The teacher's army may be small in size but it is great in faith. The Lord and His ministering angels will fight the Romans and again free the Jewish people to practice their faith.

The next morning, the teacher enters the courtyard of the Temple in Jerusalem. His message of revolt against Rome has attracted a following. Those who listen to him are inspired, but their fear is palpable. They unquestionably loathe the Romans, but too many so-called messiahs and their followers have already died. Too much righteous blood has been spilled. Several decades earlier, the Romans had crushed the Jewish monarchy and made it a capital crime for anyone to claim the mantle of Jewish kingship. The danger is real. But in spite of it all, here they behold a man unafraid of Emperor Tiberius and his bloodthirsty underling, Pontius Pilate.

After condemning Roman leadership, the teacher also rails against the corruption in the Temple. Roman influence is so deeply ingrained that it is now the Romans who appoint the chief priest. Here, in God's holiest house, the priests themselves serve as agents of Rome, colluding, conspiring, and eagerly performing their masters' nefarious bidding.

Hearing this charismatic teacher's biting invective, the fearful priests begin to murmur among themselves. A new messianic pretender has arrived from troublesome Galilee to foment a bloody rebellion among the people. Something must be done.

His sermons escalate. The teacher intends to win over the Jewish leaders, the priests, and especially the Pharisaic rabbis. He is himself a Pharisee and knows that without the support of his rabbinic colleagues he cannot hope to win the complete allegiance of the people. The rabbis respect the teacher's achievements and view him as an impressive scholar and visionary. But, as with messianic claimants of the past, they would prefer to wait and see. The rabbis hope he succeeds in his mission. They offer him moral support, but the ultimate test of his messiahship is his success. If the Romans are defeated and the prophecies fulfilled, he must indeed be their long-awaited messiah.

Then, calamity strikes. Just as the teacher's preaching in the public squares of Jerusalem reaches its crescendo, reports of the rabble-rouser reach the ears of the Jewish high priest. His minions are corrupt priests and other traitors ever on the alert for troublemakers seeking to agitate against their Roman overlords. The chief enforcer of Rome among the Jews, the high priest serves as the emperor's muscle and can scarcely afford a rebellion in Jerusalem for which he will be held accountable. In time for Passover and the thousands who come to the Temple to celebrate it, a network of spies has been established to expose subversives. Before the rabbi can mount his revolt, Roman centurions suddenly seize him at the behest of the high priest.

Without so much as a trial or hearing, the Romans lead the rabbi to the same death that awaits all political rebels: crucifixion. Just like that, it is over. A great man is dead. A brutal empire continues its oppression.

THE RESPONSE

The leader is dead. Just as his following had begun to take hold, its heart is uprooted and destroyed.

His followers are devastated. The rabbi was going to defeat the Romans, reestablish Jewish sovereignty, and usher in the end of days. To them he seemed as if sent from heaven. But the Roman machine dispatched him with such alacrity that the rabbi's followers can scarcely make sense of the tragedy. So many questions remain unanswered as they grapple with searing grief.

When the bitterness of mourning comes to an end, his followers debate the meaning of the rabbi's mission and their own future. They remain devout Jews. They believe in the Torah. They believe in the prophets. And most of all, they believe in their rabbi. How could God have allowed him to die so suddenly and with so much suffering? Why would He have permitted such a cruel execution of their righteous leader?

They debate among themselves, they grieve; but they live on in hope, studying their rabbi's teachings and devoting themselves to Torah.

In time their numbers diminish. Their group, once so large, dwindles to a desperate few as disciples abandon the cause. After all, having failed to redeem his people, the rabbi could not very well have been the messiah. He was well intentioned, bold, unique, and surely a great man, but not the promised one.

A precious few followers continue meeting in secret. They still long for freedom and despise Roman rule. Agents of Rome harass them for remaining disciples of a pariah. They must hide their rebellious ideas or face execution themselves.

The legacy of the rabbi has little future. Persecuted by Rome, devastated after the loss of their beloved leader, the teacher's followers become fewer and fewer.

ENTER THE STRANGER

Without warning, a mysterious stranger arrives. He presents himself to the teacher's remaining followers. They fear he has been sent only to harass them further; perhaps he is in the employ of the high priest, an agent of Rome, his job to undermine any and all sedition against the emperor. Yet he claims to be on the side of the rabbi's followers.

He admits he has never met the teacher, but has nonetheless become strangely enamored with the rabbi's story. Followers of the teacher had fled to Damascus, he tells the disciples, and he had been on his way there to persecute them when the fallen rabbi appeared to him in a vision. The experience changed him. He now hopes to follow the rabbi's teachings – though as the disciples will soon learn, his agenda is very different.

With a strong mystical bent, the mysterious stranger begins to reinterpret the mission of the rabbi. He shocks the devoted disciples by suggesting the rabbi was more than a man, more even than the messiah. He suggests the rabbi was outright divine – literally, the son of God. The stranger ascribes a meaning to the rabbi's death that the original followers never could. The rabbi did not die in vain, the stranger argues. His demise constituted part of his mission from God, the fulfillment of an ancient, divine plan. The rabbi had been sent to die for the sins of mankind. Without his death, all humanity would have been eternally condemned for its sins.

Furthermore, the rabbi came to this earth on a spiritual mission rather than a political one. His purpose involved not freedom from Rome but rebellion against a corrupt Jewish establishment and Torah observance that had calcified into an obstacle to salvation. The rabbi came to save the souls of men, not their persons nor their state. He lived to end the tyranny of Satan, not the rule of Rome. He came to inaugurate a new religion, not to reinforce old spiritual truths. His death served as the ultimate atonement for the iniquity of humankind. And then the stranger tells the stunned disciples that their rabbi's death brought all the laws of the Torah to completion. His execution abrogated all obligations specified in the Law.

The disciples are dumbfounded. No teaching could have given greater shock to a Jewish system. The Torah is not eternal? The rabbi was God Himself? *Impossible.* The small collection of disciples – devout Jews all – banish the stranger. Undaunted, he disseminates his theory of the rabbi's identity among the gentile Romans, launching his campaign at a most opportune time.

Roman decadence has become so corrosive and all-encompassing that the people yearn for spiritual invigoration. They long to be cleansed in a way their pagan religion cannot offer. The idea of a divine man has strong appeal. After the familiar cult of the emperor, it's easy to conceive of a man being the son of God.

The stranger's claim about the teacher dying for their sins is just as compelling. Salvation is available to all, if they only believe. Even before the rabbi appeared, 10 percent of the entire Roman Empire consisted of "Judaizers," practicing a form of Jewish spirituality. So primed, the Roman populace welcomes an expansion of Jewish-based beliefs, this time with the added convenience of faith, rather than ritual, being paramount. The new message suits their predisposition. It spreads quickly with unprecedented enthusiasm.

RISE OF A NEW FAITH

Many new adherents flock to the stranger's attractive message. The people delight in the idea of an invisible, all-powerful, personal god willing to heed individual prayers, while they balk at what seems a vast number of laws and restrictions demanded by the Jewish God.

In a move that seems designed to generate maximum popular appeal, the stranger offers up a Jewish God stripped of Jewish ritual. Salvation results from good faith rather than good acts. Moreover, the stranger combines the Roman-Hellenistic belief in man-gods with the Jewish belief in an invisible god, arguing there is a father-god, transcendent and invisible, and a son-god, earthly and human. The stranger's advocacy of the divine nature of the rabbi resonates widely.

As the stranger brings more and more new followers to a small church in Jerusalem, the rabbi's remaining disciples bristle in protest.

Their rabbi lived, taught, and died a zealous Jewish patriot. He hated the Roman Empire and Romans in general. More than anything else, he had charged his followers to strictly adhere to the Torah.

Now, in defiance of the teacher's own words, the stranger preaches a total break from all the Torah's principles. More and more gentiles embrace the new belief-based religion. As much as the old disciples would like to distance themselves from the stranger's new ways, they find they cannot. He has brought new life to their dying movement, injecting new blood and new funds. The rabbi's disciples have long suffered in extreme poverty, and the Roman converts come with gold.

Little by little, as time passes and the influence of the stranger percolates through the rabbi's disciples, their belief system changes. Gentile followers overtake the original Jewish disciples. The character of the entire movement transforms dramatically, no longer resembling what had begun as a pious movement within Judaism designed to throw off Roman rule.

ANOTHER REVOLT

Then, disaster strikes. Unable to endure any longer under the oppressive yoke of Rome, in 66 CE the Jews launch a large-scale revolt. After some initial success, the revolutionaries are overrun by the Romans and brutally crushed. By 70 CE the Temple and all of Jerusalem are destroyed and more than a million Jews are left dead. The Jewish nation becomes an object of hatred in the empire, and Rome systematically oppresses those who remain.

The gentile followers of the rabbi now take a dramatic step. There is no way they can survive as a group, much less flourish, if they are associated with the accursed Jews – now the most hated group in the empire after having launched a rebellion that shook the very foundation of Roman power. They purge the teacher of his Jewish identity as a political and religious expediency. The rabbi's writings, teachings, and story are heavily edited. Much gets rewritten completely. To ensure the future of their movement, they sever its Jewish roots, essentially transforming the teacher into a gentile. They revise their holy texts, still in formation and not yet canonized, making the rabbi appear hostile to the Jews and friendly to Rome.

Jesus' now-altered story reflects a passionate hostility toward the Pharisees in particular. In the new telling, the rabbi never rebelled against Roman authority but rather against his own people and his own faith. He abhorred the perfidious Jews and despised the hypocritical rabbis. His hatred runs so deep he even calls the Jews the spawn of the devil. As for the Romans, why, he preached outright subservience to the rule of the emperor. "Render unto Caesar that which is Caesar's," he thundered. He came not as a political leader to cast off the rule of Rome, but as a spiritual leader to cast off the rule of the Pharisees.

The editing process is haphazard and uncoordinated. Much of the original story unintentionally remains hidden in the margins. Since the writings about the rabbi evolve over many decades, individual texts conflict, allowing for the real story to be read between the lines. But the rabbi's anti-Roman views are sufficiently sanitized and enough changed that a new religion is formed, and a patriot of the Jewish people is torn and exiled from his nation.

CHAPTER 2

ROMANS AND JEWS

For all that the New Testament tells us about Jesus' epoch, it's hard
to picture it clearly. That's to be expected. From a remove of two
thousand years, it's difficult to envision anything with clarity.

To begin to imagine the character of his times, we must come to
grips with two civilizations, one long dead, the other still alive but
much changed: the Roman Empire and the Jews. As Hyam Maccoby points out in his book *Revolution in Judaea*,[3] no two peoples
were more unlike in all the ancient world. The Romans celebrated
conquest; their poets and orators praised military prowess. The Jews
championed justice, and their prophets preached an eventual era of
eternal peace.

Roman urban life centered on the cruelties of the arena with its
gory spectacles, while the Jews looked toward their Temple of God
in Jerusalem. The Romans had gods of their own, but these gods
were not so different from the men who worshipped them – lustful,
proud, wrathful, vain, and as crude as the Romans themselves.

Moral ambiguity ran deep in Roman culture. According to legend, the city of Rome was founded by the twin brothers Romulus
and Remus, who had been abandoned in the wilderness as infants
and raised by a she-wolf. As they began work on the foundations of
the city, they had an argument. Romulus killed his brother, whereupon twelve vultures appeared – a good omen. The city was named
Rome, after the victorious brother. In other words, Rome owed its
very existence to scavengers, pack hunters, and fratricide.

The city grew, and true to its violent origins, its people developed a powerful army that craved conquest. As the empire expanded and the Romans became masters of the civilized world, they absorbed the Hellenistic culture prevalent at the time. They added a new wrinkle to the brutal legend of Romulus and Remus: the people of Rome descended from Aeneas, hero of the Trojan War. They tried to veil their barbaric origins with Grecian grace. But Rome's beastly nature revealed itself in the sadistic exhibitions of the gladiators who massacred one another before cheering, bloodthirsty spectators.

The Romans never strayed far from their roots. They only covered them with a topsoil of civilization. As Maccoby puts it, "In Rome, Cicero might make speeches in the accents of Demosthenes, or Virgil sing in golden hexameters of the civilizing mission of Rome, but in Judea the meaning of Rome was the vulture and the wolf."[4]

The Jews had humble beginnings. When famine struck Canaan, Jacob's family relocated to Egypt – the only land in the region unafflicted, as the Nile continued to flow from the mountains of Sudan. At first Jacob's children were the guests of Pharaoh, who even appointed Jacob's son Joseph as his viceroy. But their station changed quickly.

A mere generation later the sons of the original Israelites were laboring in Egyptian rock quarries. To rescue them, God sent Moses, a redeemer who led the Jews into the desert toward freedom and the holy land promised to their ancestors.

Long before the two cultures collided, the differences between Jews and Romans could not have been sharper. Rome was founded in bloodshed, and through bloodshed carved a niche for itself in history. The Romans saw themselves as the center and supreme masters of the world. In contrast, the Jews envisioned a world free from the roles of slave and master, where one day the wolf would lie down with the lamb, and justice and equality would exist for all. The

Jews clung to this vision of a better and more just future through centuries of oppression and hardship.

The Jews planned to fulfill their vision through the intervention of God, not warfare. God's deliverance would arrive at the right time, preceded by the steady and continuous efforts of man to improve. Moral endeavor, personal goodness, and the betterment of society would pave the way for a messiah, who would bring eternal peace.

For this very reason Jews were unable to retreat into their culture when the Romans attacked. Years before, the Greeks had also found themselves unable to resist Roman military power; they could only surrender. Yet to them power did not matter. They could maintain their culture even without sovereignty. But for the Jews, Roman brutality and militarism represented the opposite of the eternal peace that their messiah was meant to usher in. The ensuing years under Roman rule would be difficult.

In Jesus' time Roman rule was still a relatively recent phenomenon. In 67 BCE, a century before Jesus' death, the Roman general Pompey marched on Jerusalem at the head of an army fifty thousand strong. It was one of the largest armies ever seen in the Middle East. After a brief siege, Pompey was victorious.

Accompanied by a group of soldiers, he set upon the Temple compound. The priests tried to block his path. The sanctuary was considered by the Jews as one of the holiest places on earth; most Jews were not even permitted inside. Unfazed, Pompey cut down the priests and entered the Holy of Holies, desecrating the sanctity of God's Temple.[5] This was but a premonition of things to come.

The Romans had won a valuable expanse of territory. Now, they would need to govern it. They named the land Palestine after the Philistines, who had lived in the region alongside the Jews a millennium before. After Pompey's battle-seasoned phalanxes swept through Israel, they turned homeward to Rome, leaving a power-hungry man, Hyrcanus, in charge of the region. The smaller province, Judea, came to be ruled first by Antipater, then his son, the infamous Herod. Political machinations, both Roman and Jewish, would prove common and disastrous in the coming years.

CHAPTER 3

THE PHARISEES, THE SADDUCEES, AND THE ZEALOTS

During the time of Jesus, Jews were divided primarily into two political and religious factions: the Pharisees and Sadducees. Differentiating between these groups is crucial to understanding the truth about Jesus.

While the Pharisees were committed to the Oral Law – a tradition that reached back to Moses himself – the Sadducees rejected it. They relied instead on their own literal understanding of the biblical text. Then as now, a truly literal implementation of the law was nearly impossible given the Torah's many obscure instructions. Where the Torah says punishment must be "an eye for an eye," the Sadducees rejected the rabbinic tradition that holds this refers to monetary compensation. They instead took it literally. Because the Torah forbids kindling fire on the Sabbath, the Sadducees spent nights sitting in the dark. In contrast, the Pharisees abided by the ancient tradition that disallowed only *lighting* fires on the Sabbath – and they prepared candles on Friday afternoon as part of their Sabbath observance. Orthodox Jews today uphold the Talmud, the chief document of the Pharisees. The Sadducees no longer exist and have no equivalent modern counterpart.

There were also important political differences between the Pharisees and Sadducees. While Pharisees opposed Rome, the Sadducees tended to be aristocrats who accommodated the Roman occupation. The Sadducees had made their peace with the Roman occupiers and in return, the Romans gave them positions of authority over the rest of the Jews. One such powerful position was the high priesthood, which the Roman authorities made certain was occupied by a Sadducee at all times.

Based on these facts, the differences between Pharisees and Sadducees seem fairly clear-cut. The Pharisees were loyal to Jewish tradition, the Sadducees loyal to their Roman masters. This does not, however, match the image received from scriptural sources. If we look only to the New Testament, the picture conveyed of the Pharisees resembles nothing so much as the vicious caricatures of Jews that would later populate medieval works.[6]

In the Gospels, the Pharisees and Sadducees are frequently described as acting in concert. Matthew portrays a scene in which "many of the Pharisees and Sadducees" came to be baptized by John the Baptist. Eliding the differences between them, John the Baptist rebukes both parties alike for imagining they could "flee from the coming wrath" by an extrinsic baptism of water, while their hearts remained sinful and unrepentant.[7]

How could this be? The Pharisees and Sadducees were diametrically opposed, both religiously and politically. Yet Matthew has John the Baptist denouncing them as though they were one and the same. And this doesn't even address the fact that the Pharisees and Sadducees would *never* have gone together to see John the Baptist in the first place.

Later in the Book of Matthew, Jesus himself denounces the two groups. When his disciples forget to bring bread, Jesus warns them, "Be on your guard against the yeast of the Pharisees and Sadducees." Using a parable, he describes both parties as hypocritical and arrogant, bloated by their vices in much the same way yeast causes bread to rise.[8] Anyone who lived during that era would have known the Pharisees and Sadducees were as different from one another as chalk and cheese. So why are they maligned as equal enemies of Jesus' efforts? Something is amiss. Somewhere along the line, the image of the Pharisees has been tampered with.

This is just one of many indications of a concerted effort by the editors of the Gospels to paint the Pharisees and Sadducees as having common interests. The goal of these editors will be addressed in later chapters. For now, suffice it to say that this characterization is transparently false. The Pharisees were on the side of the Jews, and the Sadducees allied with the Romans. Their interests could not have been more in conflict.

This is not to say that criticism of the Sadducees was not present in the original text. It very likely was. Jesus probably did defy the wishes of the Sadducees; it makes perfect sense that he would have opposed the puppets of Rome. But where the original versions of the Gospels surely criticized the Sadducees, we can only conclude that subsequent editors added the Pharisees in order to distance Jesus from rabbinic Judaism. Furthermore, as we shall discuss later in greater depth, all allegations that the Pharisees or their supreme court, the Sanhedrin, were involved in Jesus' death were deliberate misrepresentations.

Even insight into the Pharisees and Sadducees cannot admit us wholly into Jesus' world. We cannot understand what Jesus was really like without understanding the culture of Jewish resistance that was another important aspect of his life and times.

THE ZEALOTS

Formal Jewish resistance against the Romans began immediately after Herod's death in 4 CE. It took the form of guerilla movements such as those of Menachem of Gush-Chalav and Yehuda of Galilee. During this period, as Herod's son Archelaus waited for Rome to confirm his appointment to power, Yehuda captured the Galilee's capital and held it until the Roman governor of Syria burned it to the ground. Yehuda escaped and continued his fight as a leader of a resistance group known as the Zealots.

The Zealots took their name from a verse in Numbers recalling Pinchas, a man who was "zealous for the honor of his God."[9] They, too, were fervent for God's honor and refused to sit idly by as a foreign presence defiled His land. Though no nation had successfully resisted the Romans, the Zealots refused to back down. They hoped to weary the Romans with guerilla warfare as the Maccabees had done against the Seleucid Greeks some two hundred years before. They fought with utter tenacity.

Just as a tradition linking Pinchas to Elijah held that as a reward for his bravery Pinchas was blessed with eternal life,[10] the Zealots considered their aims messianic. Their zeal was such that they planned to drive the Romans out of their land and establish the Kingdom of God in Jerusalem. These intentions did not go unnoticed.

The Romans recognized the inherent threat of "kings of the Jews," men the Zealots and others before them had hoped to become. They routinely crucified such self-proclaimed messiahs. Men like Theudas (44 CE) and Benjamin the Egyptian (60 CE) were only the most famous of the many pretenders who died for their aspirations. Another popular rebel leader, Judas, was caught by the Romans and executed on the spot. Being a rebel against Rome in Jesus' time meant the potential for a swift and terrible death.

Years after Jesus' crucifixion, Jewish frustration with the brutal and acquisitive Romans reached a fever pitch. During his short reign from 37 to 41 CE, Emperor Caligula threatened to destroy the Temple in Jerusalem and decimate the Jewish population. Though he died before he could make good on his threats, even the most moderate Jews realized they were in danger if another madman like Caligula rose to power. Knowing the Romans, it would only be a matter of time.

In 66 CE, after a Roman procurator stole silver from the Temple, Zealots assembled a group of insurgents that rose up in defiance. Their "Great Revolt" successfully fended off a garrison of Roman soldiers. Flush with victory, they believed they would be able to defeat the Romans at last and liberate the Jews from foreign rule.

But this was not to be. By 70 CE, the Zealots' revolt came to a bloody end. Four years of ferocious fighting in the greatest rebellion against Rome to date ended in the decimation of the Jewish armies and the destruction of Jerusalem and the Temple. Rome's legions vanquished the Zealots and massacred the Jews in the Galilee and Jerusalem, killing perhaps one million people in the process. The Holy Temple was burned to the ground. It was an unspeakable tragedy for the Jewish people, and completely typical of merciless Roman political strategy.

The story of the fallen Jesus shares many of the elements of the Zealots' struggle for freedom: the utter commitment, intimations of immortality, communication of God's will to Israel and the world, impending threat of a brutal execution, and an important role in establishing the Kingdom of God in Jerusalem. The Zealot's Great Revolt would play a part in how Jesus' story was passed down. Making sense of what ultimately happened to Jesus and Christianity itself relies on understanding the interplay between fierce Zealots, devious Sadducees, and the loyal Pharisees.

CHAPTER 4

JESUS THE RABBI

Remembered as having lived his life as a carpenter, Jesus, the founder of Christianity, was also a rabbi (strange as it seems to modern ears). In those days, this title was not the mark of formal ordination it is today. Rather, it was a form of respect conferred on leaders and religious teachers by popular feeling.

Jesus' occupation as a carpenter was entirely in keeping with the custom of his day. For the rabbis, teaching was a sacred duty. And they were loath to take financial support from their communities. The Talmud documents numerous examples of sages who had "blue-collar" professions so as to avoid financial dependence on their community of students. The sage Hillel, the greatest scholar of his generation, was a bricklayer. The great Rabbi Yochanan was a shoemaker. To earn a living solely as a rabbi was deemed impious. At Mount Sinai, God gave His Law to all mankind. It was considered exploitive to sell what is, after all, the property of everyone. Jews disapproved of those who profited from people's desire to hear and understand God's instructions for living happily, peacefully, and prosperously.

Even as late as the Middle Ages, the fabled sage Rashi was a vintner, and the famed Maimonides, author of the *Guide to the Perplexed* and considered by many (including myself) the greatest Jewish sage of all time, was a court physician. It should not surprise us then that Jesus had a simple job like woodworking – just as it shouldn't surprise us that he was a rabbi.

Not only was Jesus a rabbi, he was a deeply learned, well-versed student of Jewish holy texts. Almost all his teachings derive directly from the Torah. The lessons he articulated line up squarely with Jewish morality and statements of rabbis found in the Talmud. Some of Jesus' most famous and recognizable teachings are taken directly from earlier Jewish sources.[11]

Matthew and Luke quote Jesus as saying "You cannot serve both God and money."[12] This reflects a verse in Deuteronomy in which we are told to love God with all of our "soul and strength" – which is to say, with all of our property as well.[13] Clearly, Jesus understood the verse to mean we must subject our finances to God's will, or we will find ourselves serving our purses instead of God.

His statements frequently echo the Psalms of David. In one of Jesus' most celebrated quotes he says, "Blessed are the meek, for they will inherit the earth."[14] This is a restatement of David's assertion in Psalms, "The meek will inherit the land and enjoy peace and prosperity."[15]

Jesus also draws from Jeremiah. In Matthew he is quoted as saying, "Ask and it will be given to you; seek and you will find; knock and the door will be opened to you."[16] Similarly, Jeremiah prophesies, "You will seek me and find me when you seek me with all your heart."[17]

Jesus was equally familiar with Talmudic sayings. When Jesus instructs his listeners, "First take the plank out of your own eye, and then you will see clearly to remove the speck from your brother's eye,"[18] he alludes almost word for word to a Talmudic teaching of Rabbi Tarphon: "If someone urges you to remove the speck from your eye, he must be given the answer, 'Take the plank out of your own.'"[19]

As a devout rabbi trained in the Torah, Jesus founded his sermons, parables, and aphorisms upon the same Jewish sayings and traditions that governed every aspect of his life. Yet, as telling as these lessons and sentiments gleaned from Jewish holy texts may be, they are less influential than Jesus' larger borrowings from Jewish sources, which include some of his most memorable statements of all.

THE GOLDEN RULE

It is important for Christians and Jews alike to understand that some of Jesus' most central contributions are in fact restatements of deeply Jewish traditions.

The Golden Rule is a prime example. We're all familiar with this lesson: *Do unto others as you would have others do unto you.* It's pithy, useful, easy to remember – and very Jewish in origin.

Hillel the Elder (b. 75 BCE), the greatest sage of his day, was known for his kindly disposition and the humanity of his legal rulings. He famously instructed an aspiring convert, "That which is hateful to you, do not do to your fellow."[20] With this, Hillel said, he summed up the entire Torah.

While close to the Golden Rule, critics would say it doesn't quite capture it. Some Christians have argued even the most loving Pharisee was unable to do better than a negative phrasing of the Golden Rule. They insist it took Jesus to formulate it positively.[21] Hillel, however, was only mirroring an older biblical maxim from Leviticus, "Love your neighbor as yourself," which couldn't be more affirmative.[22] Jesus repeats this verse almost exactly in the Book of Matthew: "So in everything, do to others what you would have them do to you, for this sums up the Law and the Prophets."[23] He quotes the same in the Book of Mark, as well.[24]

Jesus' famous instruction for people to love their enemies was clearly derived from a Hebrew biblical precedent. Over time, it has been augmented, its meaning expanded. Even so, the teaching derives from Exodus, where it is written: "If you come across your enemy's ox or donkey wandering off, be sure to return it."[25]

Meaning and intention grow cloudy, however, when Jesus refers
directly to the Jewish wisdom he's paraphrasing. Jesus is quoted as
claiming, "You have heard that it was said, 'Love your neighbor and
hate your enemy.'"[26] Interestingly, this statement is utterly without
Torah or Talmudic basis. Rabbinic teachings in the Midrash specifically warn against harboring grudges in the form of hatred. Indeed,
the only kind of hatred Judaism could ever condone is hatred of evil,
a subject I have elsewhere written a great deal about.

It seems later New Testament editors introduced the idea that
the Jews urged hatred of one's enemy to make Jesus' teaching stand
out with greater impact. And, as with Jesus' unlikely and unrealistic
statements depicting Pharisees and Sadducees as one and the same,
a key effect is to cast the rabbis as misguided teachers of unjust Jewish doctrine.

Clearly, it makes no sense that Jesus denigrated the precedents he
so carefully preserved. Even quotations from Jesus' Sermon on the
Mount can be traced back to Jewish teachings. The Book of Matthew quotes him as saying, "But if you do not forgive others their
sins, your Father will not forgive your sins."[27] This decisively echoes
a quotation from the Talmud: "Whose sin does He forgive? The one
who forgives transgression."[28]

While the New Testament portrays these teachings as new and
antithetical to Pharisaic instruction, they actually align perfectly
with accepted wisdom derived from the Torah. Similarly, Christians
often associate parables with Jesus to the extent that they presume
he invented a new method of teaching. This wasn't the case; parables
were a common, well-established instructional tool drawn from the
rabbinic tradition. Jesus' use of them was very much in keeping with
his role as a rabbi in a rabbinic world.[29]

THINKING LIKE A RABBI

Throughout their history, Jews have investigated and analyzed the Torah using various formal principles of interpretation. These deductive reasoning tactics apply well to the styles in which the rabbis presented law – and Jesus clearly knew them backwards and forwards.[30]

There are seven rules in total.[31] The first and most important is the *kal ve-chomer*, or "light and heavy" rule, which states it is possible to deduce from an established situation something that has yet to be ruled upon expressly. To put this in context, imagine I just purchased tires designed for difficult off-road terrain. As I'm pulling out of the parking lot onto a regular city street, a tire pops. I go back to the store and tell them I refuse to pay for the flattened tire. After all, if it is designed to withstand stone-strewn roads, *then how much more so* it should not rupture on a smooth city street. That, in a nutshell, is light-and-heavy reasoning.

The structure of this simple-to-complex reasoning – where an initial, lesser situation proves a second, more serious situation – is immediately recognizable. Religious scholar David Biven offers a straightforward example from the Midrash: "Silence becomes a scholar; how much more so a fool."[32] The idea is simple. If even a great scholar ought to know when to remain silent, how much more so an ignoramus, who has much less to offer. Notice the key phrase "how much more so," which appears in most examples of rabbinic light-and-heavy reasoning. Elsewhere, Biven quotes Rabbi Meir's analysis of Deuteronomy, "If the Scripture has thus spoken: 'I agonize over the blood of the wicked,' how much more so over the blood of the righteous that is shed?"[33]

Indeed, when we see in Jesus' teachings any variation of those words, "how much more so," it serves as a sign he is using classic rabbinic reasoning – and it's a frequent characteristic of his statements, parables, and teachings. It is to be found, for instance, in the Book of Luke, where Jesus says, "Consider the ravens: they do not sow or reap, they have no storeroom or barn; yet God feeds them. And how much more valuable you are than birds!"[34] It is present, too, in Matthew, when Jesus compares man's behavior to God's: "If you, then, though you are evil, know how to give good gifts to your children, how much more will your Father in heaven give good gifts to those who ask Him!"[35]

Biven cites a third notable passage, where "Jesus employed simple-to-complex logic to prove God's reliable care for his children. Worrying about the concerns of everyday life, Jesus warned, is distrust of God and an affront to a heavenly father who is unfailing in providing for his children." Here, Jesus' rhetoric is again classically rabbinic: "Consider how the wild flowers grow. They do not labor or spin. Yet I tell you, not even Solomon in all his splendor was dressed like one of these. If that is how God clothes the grass of the field, which is here today, and tomorrow is thrown into the fire, *how much more* will he clothe you – you of little faith!"[36]

None but a well-trained Pharisaic rabbi would draw so reliably and so heavily on the knowledge of his rabbinic predecessors in such a textbook way. And we can only conclude that Jesus was exactly that – a classically trained rabbinic scholar.

What is the most important message to take away from this chapter? Not only how much of Jesus' teaching was rooted in Pharisaic Judaism and Torah, but how similar the rabbis and Jesus sound. In many ways, Jesus and the rabbis shared both purpose and vision. Jesus was a trained rabbi, who taught like a rabbi, spoke like a rabbi, and thought like a rabbi.

CHAPTER 5

JEWISH LAW

As part and parcel of his role as a rabbi, Jesus scrupulously followed Jewish law. New Testament editors subsequently attempted to ignore this fact, claiming Jesus rebelled against Judaism. They scrambled to establish their new religion and prove that it had superseded the old, discarded Jewish faith.

In the wake of the Great Revolt of 66–70 CE, Rome was awash in anti-Semitism. Early Christians faced a quandary: they were attempting to practice and popularize a religion based on a rabbi and his teachings, during an era of unremitting anti-Jewish feeling. To preserve Christianity (and, presumably, their lives), they chose to subtly change Jesus' statements, and with them the New Testament Gospels, so as to make Jesus' teachings more palatable to gentiles.

No longer was Jesus a rabbi and Pharisee devoted to Jewish law and its preservation; he was now an original thinker, a religious rebel who defied God's law and contradicted the teachings of those who came before him, arguing that his religion was destined to replace Judaism altogether. For these New Testament editors, stitching in evidence of Jesus' defiance of Jewish law could only strengthen their case that Jesus was something apart from his rabbinical roots.

In a typical claim supporting the idea that Jesus broke from the rabbis and their traditions, the New Testament says Jesus defied the rules of the Sabbath and allowed his apostles to do likewise. This we can accept as fact. But the story isn't as simple as it seems. Jesus' supposed violation of Jewish law was in fact thoroughly in keeping with an established rabbinic idea. As evidence of Jesus' supposed law breaking, it had no force.

The story opens on the day of rest, on which God has command-ed that no man do work of any kind. As Mark tells it, "One Sabbath, Jesus was going through the grain fields and as his disciples walked along, they began to pick some heads of grain."[37] Such an act vio-lates biblical law. The New Testament does not explain the circum-stances, but observers are quick to comment on the apparent illegal-ity of what Jesus was doing. "The Pharisees said to him, 'Look, why are they doing what is unlawful on the Sabbath?'"[38] Jesus' answer to the critical "Pharisees" suggests his disciples were facing unusually difficult strain. "He answered, 'Have you never read what David did when he and his companions were hungry and in need? In the days of Abiathar the high priest, he entered the house of God and ate the consecrated bread, which is lawful only for priests to eat. And he also gave some to his companions.'"[39]

Jesus is retelling a story from the Book of Samuel in which Da-vid is fleeing from his father-in-law, Saul. Saul, convinced his son-in-law will replace him as king, is intent on murdering David before he can usurp the throne. The lives of David and his men are in dan-ger and they have no food. David allows his men to preserve their lives by eating the showbread in the tabernacle even though they are not priests and therefore forbidden from eating it under normal cir-cumstances.[40] Jesus inferred from this story that his students should be permitted to break the Sabbath and pick corn because they were on the verge of starvation.

As the early Christians would have it, Jesus committed a brave act of unorthodoxy. Jesus is quoted as saying, "The Sabbath was made for man, not man for the Sabbath."[41] This seems, on first glance, to be a clear-cut instance of Jesus flouting Jewish tradition. A deeper reading shows otherwise.

In truth, this is wholly in keeping with the Talmud, which itself says, "The Sabbath is committed to your hands, not you to its hands."[42] The Talmud establishes that people should preserve human life at virtually all costs. Religious ritual is not intended to interfere with survival, so the Sabbath should be quickly brushed aside when life is endangered.

For God, nothing is more sacred than life. The Talmud therefore accounts for situations where its own laws can be superseded. According to the laws of circumcision, surgery can be permitted on the Sabbath. The Torah commands Jews to perform the circumcision rite on the eighth day after a boy's birth. If that day is the Sabbath, the circumcision can still take place, laws against drawing blood notwithstanding. "If circumcision," explains the Talmud, "which concerns *one* of the 248 members of the body, overrides the Sabbath, shall not a man's whole body override the Sabbath?"[43] A newborn's initiation to the faith supersedes Sabbath law, and from this fact, Talmudic reasoning establishes that when necessary, any medical procedure can and must be done, even on the Sabbath.

Jesus, the studied Pharisaic rabbi, conducts his argument in the words of the Talmud: "Now if a boy can be circumcised on the Sabbath so that the Law of Moses may not be broken, why are you angry with me for healing a man's whole body on the Sabbath?"[44] Far from being proof that he was a religious rebel, this line of argument puts to rest claims he was anything other than a Pharisaic rabbi.

It bears repeating that in this situation, breaking the Sabbath did not constitute any violation at all. The rabbis wanted to save human life even at the expense of the Sabbath. Jesus and his disciples were starving to death. As rebels against Rome, Jesus and his students were probably being pursued. The fact that Jesus cites the story of King David and his men who ate the showbread evidences the fact that the disciples' lives were in jeopardy. Jesus allowed his followers to break the Sabbath to preserve life, as any other rabbi would do.

KOSHER LAW

Just as the Gospels show Jesus opposing the Sabbath, they similarly portray Jesus dismissing kosher dietary law as yet another example of his supposed defiance of Judaism. The Book of Matthew tells the story of Jesus' alleged clash with a group of Pharisees that have been nagging him about breaking with their customs – particularly a rule about washing hands before eating. Frustrated, Jesus lashes out. According to Matthew, Jesus called the crowd to him and said:

> "Listen and understand. What goes into a someone's mouth does not defile them, but what comes out of their mouth, that is what defiles them." Then the disciples came to him and asked, "Do you know that the Pharisees were offended when they heard this?" He replied, "Every plant that my heavenly Father has not planted will be pulled up by the roots. Leave them; they are blind guides. If the blind lead the blind, both will fall into a pit."[45]

With this parable, Jesus is accusing his opponents of rank stupidity and ignorance. But what is most notable of all about this passage is Jesus' famous pronouncement, "What goes into someone's mouth does not defile them, but what comes out of their mouth, that is what defiles them."[46] This has long been interpreted as a declaration that kosher laws no longer matter.

Yet this statement and its presentation are misleading. The Gospels' authors and editors have twisted Jesus' words to make him seem more rebellious against Judaism than he actually is. No wonder – in the climate following the Great Revolt of 70 CE, they had to make Christianity seem as independent of Judaism as possible.

The quote, however, was absolutely *not* an assertion that kosher laws were no longer applicable. Its source, as with most of Jesus' statements, was the Talmud. There it is written, "As the sea throws up its debris upon the shores, so the wicked have filthiness upon their mouths."[47] With this statement, both Jesus and the rabbis before him were emphasizing *lashon nekiah*, or "clean language." There are many laws in Judaism that govern what we can and cannot say – slander, gossip, and coarse language are severe sins. Jesus himself *never* ate non-kosher food. Far from denying the validity of kosher laws, Jesus was reminding his listeners of the importance of God's other laws.

Another example of this phenomenon of the Gospels' editors asserting their own agenda is where Jesus criticizes the law regarding ritual hand washing before eating bread: "When some Pharisees and teachers of the law came to Jesus from Jerusalem and asked, 'Why do your disciples break the tradition of the elders? They don't wash their hands before they eat!' Jesus replied, 'And why do you break the command of God for the sake of your tradition?'"[48]

The New Testament editors mean for us to think Jesus is defying a commandment from the Torah. But rabbis introduced this law during Jesus' own lifetime. At that time, there was still widespread debate as to its precise application and meaning. Jesus had every right to challenge it, as did other Pharisaic rabbis of his time. His participation in such a debate doesn't paint him as a rebel against his own religion. In fact, it shows just how actively involved he was in the theology of his time.

CHAPTER 6

MIRACLES

Devout Christians may be shocked to learn that even Jesus' famous miracles have precedents in biblical and rabbinic tradition. Precisely how this came to be remains unclear. Either the miracle stories were added to Jesus' biography after his death by Gospel editors who used established biblical and rabbinic miracles as models, or Jesus was a Pharisee miracle worker in the tradition of those before him. Either way, he certainly would not have offended the rabbis with his actions.

In ancient Judea, and in the northern kingdom of Galilee in particular, there was a rich tradition of rabbis who acted as miracle workers. The historian Josephus describes, for example, the famous Talmudic saint, Honi the Circle Drawer (or Onias, as Josephus called him), who gained renown for his ability to bring rain: "Now there was one whose name was Onias, a righteous man he was, and beloved of God, who, in a certain drought, had prayed to God to put an end to the intense heat, and whose prayers God had heard, and had sent them rain."[49]

WATER TO WINE

According to the Book of John, Jesus' first important miracle was to turn water into wine. It's a familiar story, but nevertheless worth repeating.[50]

On the third day a wedding took place at Cana in Galilee. Jesus' mother was there, and Jesus and his disciples had also been invited to the wedding. When the wine was gone, Jesus' mother said to him, "They have no more wine."

"Woman, why do you involve me?" Jesus replied. "My hour has not yet come."

His mother said to the servants, "Do whatever he tells you."

Nearby stood six stone water jars, the kind used by the Jews for ceremonial washing, each holding from twenty to thirty gallons. Jesus said to the servants, "Fill the jars with water"; so they filled them to the brim. Then he told them, "Now draw some out and take it to the master of the banquet."

They did so, and the master of the banquet tasted the water that had been turned into wine. He did not realize where it had come from, though the servants who had drawn the water knew. Then he called the bridegroom aside and said, "Everyone brings out the choice wine first and then the cheaper wine after the guests have had too much to drink; but you have saved the best till now." What Jesus did here in Cana of Galilee was the first of the signs through which he revealed his glory; and his disciples believed in him.[51]

No other synoptic Gospel mentions this miracle, making it difficult to confirm. But its parallels to a famous miracle in the Hebrew Bible are plainly evident. Long before Jesus, Moses' first great miracle was to turn the waters of the Nile into blood. By doing this, he established himself as a messenger of God in front of the Jews and Pharaoh.

Although we have scant details to back the story up, the resonance between the two passages is undeniable. Gospel editors may well have added Jesus' miracle after the fact as Jesus became more divine in Christian memory.

LOAVES AND FISH

In another of Jesus' miracles, he feeds a crowd with loaves and fish. This, too, has a direct precursor. The Book of Kings tells a story about the prophet Elisha feeding a hundred of his disciples with only twenty loaves of bread.

> A man came from Baal Shalishah, bringing the man of God twenty loaves of barley bread baked from the first ripe grain, along with some heads of new grain. "Give it to the people to eat," Elisha said.
>
> "How can I set this before a hundred men?" his servant asked.
>
> But Elisha answered, "Give it to the people to eat. For this is what the Lord says: 'They will eat and have some left over.'" Then he set it before them, and they ate and had some left over, according to the word of the Lord.[52]

Mark, Matthew, Luke, and John tell similar stories about Jesus, in which he feeds a few thousand of his disciples with only a few loaves of bread and some fish.[53] Matthew actually describes two seemingly separate incidents in which Jesus performs this same miracle. In the first, Jesus has been healing a crowd of sick people.

> As evening approached, the disciples came to him and said, "This is a remote place, and it's already getting late. Send the crowds away, so they can go to the villages and buy themselves some food."
>
> Jesus replied, "They do not need to go away. You give them something to eat."

"We have here only five loaves of bread and two fish," they answered.

"Bring them here to me," he said. And he directed the people to sit down on the grass. Taking the five loaves and the two fish and looking up to heaven, he gave thanks and broke the loaves. Then he gave them to the disciples, and the disciples gave them to the people. They all ate and were satisfied, and the disciples picked up twelve basketfuls of broken pieces that were left over. The number of those who ate was about five thousand men, besides women and children.[54]

In Matthew's second story, another crowd has surrounded Jesus, hoping he will heal the sick among them.

Jesus called his disciples to him and said, "I have compassion for these people; they have already been with me three days and have nothing to eat. I do not want to send them away hungry, or they may collapse on the way."

His disciples answered, "Where could we get enough bread in this remote place to feed such a crowd?"

"How many loaves do you have?" Jesus asked.

"Seven," they replied, "and a few small fish."

He told the crowd to sit down on the ground. Then he took the seven loaves and the fish, and when he had given thanks, he broke them and gave them to the disciples, and they in turn to the people. They all ate and were satisfied. Afterward the disciples picked up seven basketfuls of broken pieces that were left over. The number of those who ate was four thousand men, besides women and children."[55]

It is likely all of the Gospels were interpreting an earlier story about Jesus that had been around for years. It is even possible that the first version of the story was not meant to be taken literally. The convenient imagery of the five loaves representing the five books of the Torah suggests, as Hyam Maccoby notes, that this incident might have started as a parable Jesus related to teach a lesson.

In any case, the miracle described in the Gospels seems to be modeled after the story of Elisha in Kings. The crucial difference is that Jesus feeds a far larger crowd of people. The early Christians almost certainly amplified these stories to establish him as a prophet greater even than Elisha.[56]

WALKING ON WATER

Not even Jesus' feat of walking on water is without precedent in Jewish tradition. The stories of Jesus recounted in the Gospels that depict him walking on water and quelling storms are clear reflections of the Hebrew Bible story of Jonah, of psalm 107, and of a verse from the ninth chapter of Job.

The book of Mark relates an anecdote in which Jesus stops a storm that threatens his disciples' boat:

> A furious squall came up, and the waves broke over the boat, so that it was nearly swamped. Jesus was in the stern, sleeping on a cushion. The disciples woke him and said to him, "Teacher, don't you care if we drown?" He got up, rebuked the wind, and said to the waves, "Quiet! Be still!" Then the wind died down and it was completely calm. He said to his disciples, "Why are you so afraid? Do you still have no faith?" They were terrified and asked each other, "Who is this? Even the wind and the waves obey him!"[57]

A cursory look at the text of psalm 107 betrays clear commonalities:

> For he spoke and stirred up a tempest that lifted high the waves. They mounted up to the heavens and went down to

the depths; in their peril their courage melted away. They
reeled and staggered like drunkards; they were at their wits'
end. Then they cried out to the Lord in their trouble, and
he brought them out of their distress. He stilled the storm
to a whisper; the waves of the sea were hushed. They were
glad when it grew calm, and he guided them to their desired
haven.[58]

The narrative in Mark seems equally inspired by the story of Jonah.
Jesus is sleeping on the boat. His disciples wake him in desperation,
thinking they are going to drown. Similarly, the sailors rush to wake
Jonah thinking he might be able to save them. The Gospels used the
model established by Jonah to show Jesus' control over the seas.[59]

This turns out to be a warm-up for an even greater miracle. Mark
later describes Jesus walking on water:

> Later that night, the boat was in the middle of the lake, and
> he was alone on land. He saw the disciples straining at the
> oars, because the wind was against them. Shortly before dawn
> he went out to them, walking on the lake. He was about to
> pass by them, but when they saw him walking on the lake,
> they thought he was a ghost. They cried out, because they all
> saw him and were terrified. Immediately he spoke to them
> and said, "Take courage! It is I. Don't be afraid." Then he
> climbed into the boat with them, and the wind died down.
> They were completely amazed, for they had not understood
> about the loaves; their hearts were hardened.[60]

Likewise, Matthew explains that Jesus walked on the water and
helped Peter to do the same:

> "Lord, if it's you," Peter replied, "tell me to come to you on
> the water."

"Come," he said. Then Peter got down out of the boat, walked on the water, and came toward Jesus. But when he saw the wind, he was afraid and, beginning to sink, cried out, "Lord, save me!" Immediately Jesus reached out his hand and caught him. "You of little faith," he said, "why did you doubt?" And when they climbed into the boat, the wind died down. Then those who were in the boat worshipped him, saying, "Truly you are the Son of God."[61]

This story was written to establish Jesus' capacity to tread "on the waves of the sea," as Job 9:8 says God does. It also reflects psalm 107, in which sailors cry out to God to save them from a storm, and He answers them. The conjunction of multiple references to very specific scriptural precedents ultimately appears a bit too convenient and coincidental to have crept into the text without the judicious guidance of New Testament editors, who were clearly establishing Jesus' connection to earlier biblical prophesies and events.

CHAPTER 7

JESUS THE HEALER

Jesus' miracles as a healer are also very much in keeping with the rabbinical tradition of the Second Temple era. In the Talmud, we find many reports of cures and exorcisms performed by learned and well-respected rabbis. Far from being frightening to the Pharisees of his time, such stories about Jesus would have seemed conspicuously familiar.

Many Gospel stories describe Jesus' casting out of demons. At one point he goes so far as to declare: "But if I drive out demons by the finger of God, then the kingdom of God has come upon you."[62] This, too, is in keeping with Talmudic tradition. In myriad stories, rabbis were shown to have power over demons. In one instance, Rabbi Hanina ben Dosa is able to control and issue orders to Agrat bat Machlat, the princess of demons. "If I am of account in heaven," he says to her, "I order you never to pass through settled regions,"[63] so that she will not trouble humans. In another, Rav Acha bar Ya'akov confronts a demon occupying a study hall. "It appeared to him as a serpent with seven heads," but by praying, Rav Acha is able to fight off the beast: "Every prostration that he did removed one head."[64]

By healing the sick and rescuing them from demons, Jesus saw himself as fulfilling the prophecy of Isaiah: "Then will the eyes of the blind be opened and the ears of the deaf unstopped."[65] Doing so was clearly important to him. Jesus repeatedly extols his efforts to heal the sick and to raise his disciples' consciousness to a plane where they can see what heretofore had been obscured: "Blessed are the eyes that see what you see. For I tell you that many prophets and kings wanted to see what you see but did not see it, and to hear what you hear but did not hear it."[66]

Christians see Jesus' miraculous powers as proof that he was divine. It is not so simple for Jews. Suspension of the laws of nature is not evidence of supernatural powers – it simply uncovers a higher reality, drawing the curtain on the hand of God that not only lurks behind but constitutes the true fabric of the universe.

The Talmud itself is filled with stories of great rabbis healing the sick, even raising the dead, as in a famous story from the Babylonian Talmud: "Rabba and Rabbi Zeira celebrated their Purim feast together. They drank. Rabba arose [in a drunken stupor] and slaughtered Rabbi Zeira. The next morning he [Rabba] prayed and revived him."[67] Surely, no Jew would ascribe a divine nature to the Talmudic sage Rabba. Rather, his ability to revive the dead depended entirely on his prayer to God, the only one with the power to grant life to the deceased.

But even this is merely an echo of the famous story of Elisha, the prophet who revives a dead boy after his mother's pleading:

> When Elisha reached the house, there was the boy lying dead on his couch. He went in, shut the door on the two of them, and prayed to the Lord. Then he got on the bed and lay upon the boy, mouth to mouth, eyes to eyes, hands to hands. As he stretched himself out upon him, the boy's body grew warm. Elisha turned away and walked back and forth in the room and then got on the bed and stretched out upon him once more. The boy sneezed seven times and opened his eyes. Elisha summoned Gehazi and said, "Call the Shunammite." And he did. When she came, he said, "Take your son." She came in, fell at his feet and bowed to the ground. Then she took her son and went out.[68]

The Christian impulse to use Jesus' signs as proof that he was divine, or as the pretext for belief, seems to have frustrated even Jesus himself. "He sighed deeply and said, 'Why does this generation ask for a sign? Truly I tell you, no sign will be given to it.'"[69] On another occasion he declares with exasperation: "Unless you people see signs and wonders...you will never believe."[70]

While he wishes to heal the sick, Jesus does not want his actions to be interpreted as any claim to divinity. Even less so does he want the public to delight in the messenger while losing sight of the message. Jesus was spreading God's word, not his own. In multiple instances Mark relates Jesus going so far as to order those who witness his healings not to tell others.[71] He feared – rightly, as it turned out – that his followers would highlight his personality at the expense of his calling.

Even Jesus' exorcisms bear a strong similarity to those performed by rabbis of his time. As Mark writes, "So they brought him. When the spirit saw Jesus, it immediately threw the boy into a convulsion. He fell to the ground and rolled around, foaming at the mouth."[72]

Many great men of the era claimed to be able to perform exorcisms. The historian Josephus described in detail his contemporary, a Jewish exorcist named Eleazer, who had the ability to draw demons out through the nose of the afflicted. "When Eleazar would persuade and demonstrate to the spectators that he had such a power, he set a little way off a cup or basin full of water, and commanded the demon, as he went out of the man, to overturn it, and thereby to let the spectators know that he had left the man."[73] Clearly, Jesus wasn't the only exorcist at work in those times.

Among the Dead Sea Scrolls there is a description of an exorcism that is strongly reminiscent of the ones performed by Jesus. "So I prayed for him, that blasphemer, and laid my hands upon his head. Thereupon the plague was removed from him, the evil spirit exorcised from him, and he was healed."[74]

The Talmud relates many stories about exorcisms that demonstrate Jesus was firmly in line with his colleagues in performing them. Here is one such story about the great sage Rabbi Hanina ben Dosa:

> Once Rabbi Hanina ben Dosa went to immerse himself in [the water of] a cave. Kuthim [Samaritans] came and placed a large rock over the mouth of the cave. The spirits came and removed it. Subsequently, an evil spirit haunted a poor woman in Rabbi Hanina's neighborhood.
>
> His students said to him: "Rabbi, see how this poor woman suffers grief from the evil spirit."
>
> Rabbi Hanina addressed the spirit: "Why do you cause grief to the daughter of Abraham?"
>
> The spirit responded: "Are you not the one who went down to dip in the cave, and so on...till I came with my brothers and my father's household and removed the rock. Is this how you pay me for the favor I did you?"
>
> He answered her: "I decree."

The story ends abruptly here, although we are given to understand that the spirit ultimately fled, and the woman was cured.[75] This is clearly an antecedent for Jesus' own miracles. Doubtless, Jesus' most uncanny acts had roots in Jewish tradition, and as we shall soon see, there are even precursors for Jesus' most famous miraculous act: raising the dead.

RAISING THE DEAD

Strange as it may seem, Jesus' most famous miracle, raising the dead, is as much in line with biblical stories and rabbinic legends as any other. The New Testament says Jesus raised at least three people. One was a widow's son in the town of Nain. According to the Book of Luke, "As he approached the town gate, a dead person was being carried out – the only son of his mother, and she was a widow. And a large crowd from the town was with her. When the Lord saw her, his heart went out to her and he said, 'Don't cry.' Then he went up and touched the bier they were carrying him on, and the bearers stood still. He said, 'Young man, I say to you, get up!' The dead man sat up and began to talk, and Jesus gave him back to his mother."[76]

In a second story, a man named Jairus has approached Jesus, pleading for help. His daughter is deathly ill. By the time Jesus gets to his house, the girl has died. In Mark's words, "Jesus saw a commotion, with people crying and wailing loudly. He went in and said to them, 'Why all this commotion and wailing? The child is not dead but asleep.' But they laughed at him. After he put them all out, he took the child's father and mother and the disciples who were with him, and went in where the child was. He took her by the hand and said to her, 'Talitha koum!' (which means 'Little girl, I say to you, get up!') Immediately the girl stood up and began to walk around (she was twelve years old)."[77]

The third and most famous of Jesus' resurrections is that of Lazarus. To bring the dead man back to life, all Jesus needs to do is call out to him. "Jesus called in a loud voice, 'Lazarus, come out!' The dead man came out, his hands and feet wrapped with strips of linen, and a cloth around his face."[78]

All these stories are reminiscent of Elijah and Elisha's raising boys from the dead by lying on top of them and praying to God.

We have already explored Talmudic legends where rabbis resurrect the dead. But if we look more closely into the Hebrew Bible, there is even more to be found. In the Book of Kings, we are told that Elijah went to a widow's house and miraculously provided her with an unending supply of food. Afterwards, her son dies, and she blames Elijah, whereupon he performs another miracle for the widow.

"Give me your son," Elijah replied. He took him from her arms, carried him to the upper room where he was staying, and laid him on his bed. Then he cried out to the Lord, "Lord my God, have You brought tragedy even on this widow I am staying with, by causing her son to die?" Then he stretched himself out on the boy three times and cried to the Lord, "Lord my God, let this boy's life return to him!" The Lord heard Elijah's cry, and the boy's life returned to him, and he lived. Elijah picked up the child and carried him down from the room into the house. He gave him to his mother and said, "Look, your son is alive!"[79]

If Elijah, one of the greatest prophets in Jewish history, is allowed to raise people from the dead, it is no sin against God to do so. This story from Kings is also similar to that of Jesus and the widow's son in Nain.

Jesus' story, as told in the New Testament, may very well have been designed to emulate those of great Hebrew prophets before him, like Elijah. In the same spirit, his miracles can easily fit into and be interpreted in the light of Jewish tradition.

Chapter 8

Jesus Never Claimed to Be Divine

Whether or not the miracles attributed to Jesus actually occurred, what is clear is that as a devout Pharisee and rabbi, he would have been appalled at how his followers would later define him. No doubt Jesus hoped and believed he was the messiah sent by God to save his suffering people. However, he understood his own messiahship in traditional and biblical terms: He was a Jewish king who sought to eliminate Roman rule and reestablish an independent Jewish commonwealth, as in the days of his ancestor King David. He was a redeemer. But he absolutely did *not* consider himself divine.

Nearly all the expressions Christians use to prove that Jesus declared himself God are textual misunderstandings. For example, the phrase "son of man" occurs frequently. In this usage, Christian texts capitalize the word *man*, as if it refers to a deity. This is actually a common expression, employed many times by other Jewish prophets. Ezekiel, for example, uses the term repeatedly – literally translated from the Hebrew as "son of Adam," the first man. Adam was not a deity. The capitalization of the term is erroneous and misleading. By referring to himself as the "son of man," Jesus joins a longstanding tradition among Jewish prophets.

Similarly, when Jesus speaks in the first-person singular in God's name, it is not a declaration of his own divinity. Moses does the same in Deuteronomy, when he tells the Jews that if they obey the word of God, "I," Moses, will give them material wealth.[80] Prophets speaking in the name of God often sound as though they are channeling the deity. This is not to be confused with their being divine. It is commonplace for prophets not to distinguish between themselves and God in their speech. We have no reason to believe Jesus ever thought of himself as a deity. As a Jew, he surely would have regarded any such interpretation as blasphemous.

Prevailing currents in religious thought may have injected such thinking into Jesus' teachings. As Hyam Maccoby explains, Gnostic religious beliefs, which pervaded the Middle East in Jesus' era, maintained that the world was created by a demiurge, or sub-god, who was evil.[81] The true good god was too important to concern himself with human beings. These Gnostic sects believed the god of goodness would send down an incarnation of himself to lead human beings toward goodness and away from the demiurge. And this is not the only tradition of corporeal gods. Much of the Greek Pantheon included beings that were part human.

The emergence of Jesus as a deity mimicked Gnostic and pagan beliefs and began decades after his death. It culminated in the Council of Nicaea in the fourth century, when the Church declared it heretical to believe that Jesus was mortal. This gathering of men decided, some might argue almost arbitrarily, which beliefs constituted the truth about their religion's namesake. Among these ideas was that besides being wholly human, Jesus was also wholly divine – an ironic decision given the earthly and political nature of many of Jesus' central concerns.

JESUS THE POLITICIAN

From the time of Abraham, the figure of the Hebrew prophet stood at the forefront of two fights. One was against oppression, injustice, and immorality. The other was for self-determination and the actualization of one's unique potential in the service of God.

The greatest prophet was Moses, who led the Jews from slavery and the grasp of the tyrant Pharaoh to Mount Sinai so they could each hear God directly. His successors fought an array of oppressors that brutalized the innocent and the helpless. Jesus undoubtedly saw himself as part of this tradition as he protested against the Roman occupiers.

Taken at face value, the Gospels' characterization of Jesus has him unconcerned with earthly goings-on. His saintly character makes him seem oblivious to the oppression of the Jews. But how could a man such as Jesus remain so aloof? He was by all accounts a holy and wholesome man, focused on the real practice and enactment of justice. It is therefore impossible to picture Jesus without imagining his political nature.

An examination of the evidence suggests that after Jesus' death, editors removed his political diatribes against Rome from his life story. Indeed, as Hyam Maccoby insightfully notes, they removed the Romans themselves almost completely.

Think about it. The Romans were militarily occupying Judea. They had won over an entire religious faction, the Sadducees, to ensure their continued dominance in the region. They had the most powerful army in the world occupying the Holy Land. Yet where are the Romans in the Gospels? They are barely seen at all. And when they do appear, they are described as uncharacteristically virtuous and passive. The Book of Matthew tells the story of Jesus healing the servant of a Roman centurion and marveling at the man's faith. "Truly I tell you," he says to his apostles, "I have not found anyone in Israel with such great faith."[82] A Roman soldier tasked with oppressing the Jews also had great faith? Hard to believe, yet Luke expands on this idea. As the crowd exhorts Jesus to help the Roman: "This man deserves to have you do this," they say, "because he loves our nation and has built our synagogue."[83] Such a claim is beyond improbable.

Roman legionnaires were everywhere in Jerusalem and the sur-
rounding areas. It would be only a matter of decades before they
would destroy the Temple and massacre the Jewish populace with a
brutality that was perhaps second in Jewish history only to the Holocaust. Yet the New Testament insists on viewing them as benign
bystanders.

It is worth mentioning that the New Testament takes pains to
make even Pontius Pilate, a notoriously cruel despot, look blameless.
He desperately tries to persuade the Jews to let Jesus go, saying to the
crowd, "Look, I am bringing him out to you to let you know that I
find no basis for a charge against him.... You take him and crucify
him. As for me, I find no basis for a charge against him."[84] It is ultimately a Roman soldier that recognizes Jesus' divinity. As Mark tells
the story, "When the centurion, who stood there in front of Jesus,
saw how he died, he said, 'Surely this man was the Son of God!'"[85] In
almost all cases, the Romans appear to be nothing more than virtuous overseers attempting to mitigate Jewish cruelty.

This is, of course, pure fiction. The Romans were the most brutal force of the ancient world. Their choke hold over Judea was thor-
ough and crushing. Pilate himself was a mass murderer. Barely mentioning them in the story of Jesus would be the equivalent to writing
a history of Poland from 1939 to 1945 without mentioning the Nazis.
But the Romans were removed from the story, or their actions were
whitewashed whenever their role was so central it could not be delet-
ed. While the editors were set on demonstrating to their readership
that Jesus had no quarrel with the Romans, they made it clear that it
was the Jews who infuriated him and against whom he rebelled.

Jesus defended the innocent and condemned the wicked. He
drove money changers from the Temple with a whip, and declared
his objective to serve as the light of the world. He was impassioned
in his commitment to justice and extremely sensitive to the suffering of others. Yes, he would have been right to inspire the Jews of

Palestine to band together and redouble their commitment to God's Torah. The spiritual element of his quest was crucial. But as much as Jesus cared about his people's souls, he must have also cared about their safety and liberty. Let's not forget the Romans invaded Jesus' homeland to increase their glory and extract tribute from its people. Yet the Gospels, with few exceptions, do not feature criticisms of the Romans or their brutality.

The editing done to purge the crimes of the Romans and to delete references to Jesus' rebellion against them was an intricate and difficult job. Part of it was left incomplete. Remember, thousands of manuscripts were circulating around. Not all could be completely purged. Flashes of accuracy remain. "We have found this man subverting our nation. He opposes payment of taxes to Caesar and claims to be Messiah, a king."[86] This statement in Luke indicates that corrupt priests delivered Jesus to his oppressors, the Roman administration, because he was a rebel against Roman rule pure and simple. Because it is so different from other statements throughout the rest of the Gospels, which take great pains to make Jesus non-political, it is an obvious piece of real history that slipped through, contrary to the intent of editors pushing Paul's concept of a strictly spiritual Jesus.

The more we peel away the surface, the more we see the truth: Jesus, I will continue to show, was a great political leader who fought for the liberation of his people. In this sense, he saw himself in the guise of Moses and David, both of whom, while supremely concerned with the spiritual welfare of the people, were first and last concerned with the political freedom of the Jewish nation.

CHAPTER 9

THE FANTASY OF THE EVIL JEWS

Though Jesus did not believe himself divine, he did believe that he was the messiah. This meant he thought he was the long-promised messianic king that would restore Jewish political independence by throwing off the yoke of an external oppressor. This mission of political liberation – the creation of an independent Jewish nation capable of worshipping their God without the obstruction of an external oppressor – is the first and most important role of the messiah. For believing this, he paid the highest price and was crucified for political insurrection. Jesus joined the ranks of his people's martyrs, millions of whom have been prepared to die for their faith and the welfare of their people throughout history.

Once we agree that Jesus was a martyr, the more difficult question is this one: *Who killed Jesus?*

No question defines the Jewish-Christian relationship more than this one, for the Jews have long borne the brunt of being falsely listed in answer. The anti-Semitic claim that the Jews killed Jesus became the wellspring from which Christian anti-Semitism flowed, and its root is in the text of the Gospel itself. Just imagine the enormity of the charge. The Jews are accused of being possessed of such infinite demonic power that they were capable of murdering God Himself, snuffing out the ultimate source of life and light. Only a truly savage and dark nation, enemies of the deity and all holiness, could be capable of even attempting – let alone succeeding in – exterminating the Creator.

Portions of the New Testament seem to suggest quite clearly that the Jews in Jesus' time possessed such deep, demonic power that they were ready, willing, and able to murder God incarnate. From this allegation emerged the image of Jews and Judaism as agents of Satan, sworn enemies of God. In the long annals of history, has any nation or individual ever been accused of something more serious than killing the source of all that is? Just how monstrous must one be to snuff out the very light of the universe, plunging humanity into a hell of eternal darkness? All the anti-Semitic caricatures of the Jews manipulating banks and the media and intent on conquering the world itself stem from this charge. The Jews are jealous of God and His power, and wish to claim all for themselves. They are voracious and insatiable. They will destroy and consume all who stand in their way, including the Creator Himself. The damage done by this abominable slander over the past two millennia is so great that it is simply too large to accurately reckon.

The truth is that the Jews did not kill Jesus, nor did they want him dead. The Roman government did, and it was they who dispatched him with great alacrity once he was perceived as a threat.

The Myth That the Jews Killed Jesus

The myth that the Jews killed Jesus has become so ingrained in our culture that even many contemporary Christians accept it as axiomatic. In the introduction to *Our Hands Are Stained with Blood*, a book that proposes to condemn anti-Semitism, my friend the Jewish convert to Christianity, scholar Dr. Michael Brown, with whom I have debated Christianity and Jesus in high-profile debates more than twenty times, can't help but write, "I am convinced that international Christian repentance for the Church's past (and present) sins against the Jews will lead to international Jewish repentance for Israel's past (and present) sins against Jesus."[87]

This is simply amazing. Even in a book written to condemn historical Christian Jew-hatred, the author thinks nothing of condemning Jewish "sins" against Jesus, that is, the Jews' rejection of Jesus and their turning him over to the Romans and demanding that he be crucified. Brown believes Jews still bear the blame for Jesus' death, but nevertheless Christians should not be anti-Jewish. His reasoning posits first that the perception of anti-Semitism prevents other Jews from potentially converting to Christianity. And second, even if the Jews are guilty of killing Jesus, they must be forgiven and brought to a belief in Jesus, since Jesus ultimately laid down his life for the atonement of human sin and was therefore complicit in the Jewish act of slaughter. This is truly a disheartening – and self-defeating – line of thinking.

Jacques-Benigne Bossuet, the influential seventeenth-century French orator and bishop, said the following about Jewish culpability in the death of Jesus: "I hear the Jews crying out, 'His blood falls on us and our children' (Matthew 27:25). There it shall be, a cursed race! Your prayer will be answered more than amply. His blood will pursue you and your last offspring until the Lord, grown tired of His vengeance, will remember, at the end of time, your miserable remnants.... According to God's hidden counsel, the Jews will survive in the midst of the nations...banished from the Promised Land, having no land to cultivate, slaves wherever they are, without honor, without freedom, without the appearance of a people!"[88]

Bossuet's brand of theological justification for inflicting suffering and slaughter on Jews has survived into the modern era. It served as the principal justification for the Catholic Church's refusal to formally recognize the State of Israel until 1993.[89] The Church could not accept a reconstituted Jewish sovereignty because their worldview relied, even in the modern age, upon imagining the Jews to be accursed, dangerous, outsiders, rebels, sneaks, and a host of other smears that allowed the Church to orient itself as the center of the good and right world.

Many anti-Semitic commentators would not be satisfied until the Jews of today express sorrow or shame for what, in their eyes, the Jews of antiquity had done. Ernest Renan, the French Orientalist and author of *Life of Jesus*, wrote, "According to our modern ideas, there is no transmission of moral demerit from father to son; no one is accountable to human or divine justice except for that which he himself has done.... But nations, like individuals, have their responsibilities, and if ever crime was the crime of a nation, it was the death of Jesus."[90] For Renan, the Jews as a nation can and do have the eternal mark of guilt upon them. Yet, somehow, the modern Christian cannot blame the individual modern Jew. In response, Renan enunciates a strange paradox, as if saying to the Jew, "You as yourself are blameless, but you in your heritage and identity are demonic." Renan, like so many others, wants Jews to feel ashamed and guilty. He wants the individual Jew to renounce Judaism for Christianity, and by doing so presumably escape the blame for Jesus' execution.

This line of thinking is not a modern innovation – it can be found in the words of one of the greatest Christian Church fathers, Augustine of Hippo. In his poisonous words, "The Jews held Jesus, they insulted him; the Jews bound him; they crowned him with thorns, dishonored him by spitting on him; they scourged him; they heaped abuse upon him; they hung him on a tree; they pierced him with a lance."[91] This quotation became popular in Easter sermons in churches, and these very sermons often led to pogroms in Jewish communities.

Augustine wrote extensively about the fate of the Jews on earth. "The Church admits and avows the Jewish people to be cursed," he wrote in a letter, "because after killing Christ they continue to till the ground of an earthly circumcision, an earthly Sabbath, an earthly Passover, while the hidden strength or virtue of making known

Christ, which this tilling contains, is not yielded to the Jews while they continue in impiety and unbelief, for it is revealed in the New Testament. While they will not turn to God, the veil which is on their minds in reading the Old Testament is not taken away...the Jewish people, like Cain, continue tilling the ground, in the carnal observance of the law, which does not yield to them its strength, because they do not perceive in it the grace of Christ."[92]

He manages to be incredibly cruel even when he urges Christians not to outright murder Jews: "Not by bodily death shall the ungodly race of carnal Jews perish. For whoever destroys them in this way shall suffer sevenfold vengeance, that is, shall bring upon himself the sevenfold penalty under which the Jews lie for the crucifixion of Christ. So to the end of the seven days of time, the continued preservation of the Jews will be a proof to believing Christians of the subjection merited by those who, in the pride of their kingdom, put the Lord to death."[93] According to this vision, the Jews should not be killed so that their presence can serve as testimony to God's disfavor: they will forever live their lives as second-class citizens.

John Chrysostom (ca. 344–407 CE), a saint in the eyes of the Catholic Church, became one of the significant early instigators of intense hatred against Jews. He declared:

> No Jew adores God!... The Jews themselves are demons.... In their synagogue stands an invisible altar of deceit on which they sacrifice not sheep and calves but the souls of men.... They live for their bellies, they gape for the things of this world, their condition is not better than that of pigs or goats because of their wanton ways and excessive gluttony. They know but one thing: to fill their bellies and be drunk.... Shun the evil gatherings of the Jews and their synagogues, both in the city and in the suburbs, because these

are robbers' dens and dwellings of demons.... The Jews are more savage than any highwaymen.[94]

According to this so-called saint, the Jews possess magical powers and perform strange demonic rites of an almost cannibalistic nature. The people who raised and listened to Jews, says Chrysostom, are utterly earthly and animalistic. Their code of living espouses a conduct of crime and bestial behavior. Chrysostom's scathing rhetoric makes his message crystal clear: *Fear the Jews*. Fear them to your core. Fear them, hate them, and do not doubt that they will kill you to satisfy themselves. He transforms the Jews into something out of his personal fantasy of evil and excess, a living blight upon the earth that his personal Jesus came to save.

Even Thomas Aquinas (1225–1274), arguably the greatest Catholic intellectual of all time, preached that the Jewish people were damned for killing Jesus, and could only be saved by renouncing their faith and accepting baptism. "They should be compelled by the faithful, if at all possible to do so," Aquinas wrote, "so that they do not hinder the faith, by their blasphemies, or by their evil persuasions, or even by their open persecutions. It is for this reason that Christ's faithful often wage war with unbelievers."[95]

If anything, the Protestant Reformation made the situation even worse. In his work *On the Jews and Their Lies*, Martin Luther preached:

> [Christians should] set fire to their synagogues or schools and to bury and cover with dirt whatever will not burn, so that no man will ever again see a stone or cinder of them.... I advise that [Jewish] houses also be razed and destroyed. For they pursue in them the same aims as in their synagogues. Instead they might be lodged under a roof or in a barn, like the gypsies. This will bring home to them the fact that they are not masters in our country, as they boast, but that they

are living in exile and in captivity, as they incessantly wail
and lament about us before God.[96]

By the time of Hitler's Holocaust, two thousand years of Christian
hatred toward Jews made it easy for Europeans to look the other
way, or even actively assist as Nazis slaughtered the Jews en masse.
Rabbi Michael Dov-Ber Weissmandel escaped from deportation to
Auschwitz and approached the papal nuncio for help in stopping the
extermination of Slovakian Jews. The Catholic archbishop replied,
"There is no innocent blood of Jewish children in the world. All Jewish blood is guilty. You have to die. This is the punishment that has
been awaiting you because of that sin [the murder of Jesus]."[97]

The Catholic Church's tragic refusal at the papal level to make
a public stand and commit itself to saving Jewish lives during Hitler's Holocaust was all too consistent with the Church's historical in-
difference to Jewish suffering. Pius XII was pope of the worldwide
Catholic Church from 1939 until 1958, and was the first foreign dig-
nitary to reach an accord with Nazi Germany after Hitler took power. It would be a stretch to refer to this deeply anti-Semitic pope as
"holy" father. British journalist John Cornwell chronicled the life of
Pope Pius in his international best seller *Hitler's Pope*. Before ascend-
ing to the papacy, Pius, then Cardinal Eugenio Pacelli, signed a con-
cordat with Nazi Germany; this was seven months after Adolf Hitler
had been appointed chancellor of Germany. As papal nuncio, Pacelli directly negotiated with Hitler, and Hitler praised Pacelli's treaty
for being "especially significant in the urgent struggle against international Jewry."

His papal record was just as tragic. After Pacelli was named pope
in 1939, he shelved a papal encyclical condemning the outbreak of
anti-Semitism in Germany that had been prepared by his predeces-
sor, Pius XI. He refrained from condemning the Holocaust during
the six years in which six million Jews, and millions of others in

Europe, were systematically detained, deported, incarcerated, and exterminated. In 1942 he refused to sign an Allied condemnation of Germany's systematic destruction of European Jews despite extensive pressure to do so. He actively flattered Hitler, courting his favor, writing him letters in which he praised him, referring to him as "the illustrious Hitler." He also saw fit to turn Hitler's birthday into a de facto holiday. As Cornwell writes, "On April 20, 1939, at Pacelli's express wish, Archbishop Orsenigo, the nuncio in Berlin, opened a gala reception at Hitler's fiftieth birthday. The birthday greetings thus initiated by Pacelli immediately became a tradition. Each April 20 during the few fateful years left to Hitler and his Reich, Cardinal Bertram of Berlin was to send 'warmest congratulations to the Führer in the name of the bishops and the diocese in Germany,' to which he added 'fervent prayers which the Catholics of Germany are sending to heaven on their altars.'"[98]

In December 2004, evidence surfaced that Pius had specifically ordered Church authorities not to return Jewish children to their rightful guardians after World War II had ended. In October 1946, Jewish parents came knocking on church doors to retrieve children secreted away in Catholic guardianship during the Holocaust. In response, the Vatican sent its instructions to the papal nuncio in France, Cardinal Angelo Roncalli, who later became Pope John XXIII. Roncalli was a man of known compassion for Jews – he had been working to reunite Jewish children hidden in Catholic institutions with their parents, relatives, and Jewish organizations. However, this papal letter ordered Roncalli to desist: "Those children who have been baptized cannot be entrusted to institutions that are unable to ensure a Christian education."[99]

Pope Pius insisted on depriving Jewish parents of their own children. "If the children have been entrusted [to the Church] by their parents, and if the parents now claim them back, they can be returned, provided the children themselves have not been baptized. It should be noted that this decision of the Congregation of the Holy Office has been approved by the Holy Father." The Church's authoritative Congregation deliberated and decided on this monstrous policy of refusing to return baptized Jewish children to their parents. And the pope himself personally approved it.[100]

Robert Katz's *The Battle for Rome* convincingly demonstrates that Pius collaborated with the Nazi government in their occupation of Rome and did nothing to stop the rounding up of Jews for extermination at Auschwitz. Pius was informed every step of the way as the Germans, on October 16, 1943, collected more than one thousand Jews of Rome, nearly all of whom would perish in gas chambers a few days later at Auschwitz. A special SS contingent was brought in for the roundup. Many of them had never before seen the great city, and they used this action as a partial tourist excursion. They brought the Jews to St. Peter's Square, and herded them into open trucks parked not more than three hundred feet from Pius's window. Pius offered no protest and upheld a scandalous policy of strict neutrality while the Germans in his diocese literally turned the people of Jesus into ash.

Pius granted a secret audience to Supreme SS Polizeiführer Wolff, Himmler's former chief of staff, serving in 1943 as the chief of German persecution apparatus in occupied Italy. The meeting took place in strict confidence, and Wolff came dressed in disguise. Years later, Wolff said of the meeting: "From the Pope's own words I could sense the sincerity of his sympathy and how much he loved the German people."

But while he may not have prized the lives of Jews, Pius held the bricks and mortar of his churches in high esteem. As the British and American armies geared up for a massive offensive in the spring of 1944, Pius suddenly found his voice. He condemned the Allies for bombing the Eternal City and ordered his American bishops to launch public relations offensives in the United States to pressure the Roosevelt administration to preserve the sacred monuments of the city. This, while the Nazis were gassing more than fifteen thousand Jews per day.

These horrific details make abundantly clear that despite his white robes, Pius was an unholy soul whose beatification, now under consideration by the Church, would be a sin against God, a stain upon Christianity, and an affront to the memory and teachings of the Jewish freedom fighter whom he worshipped, Jesus.

But we cannot be shocked at the pope's actions nor the history of Christian anti-Semitic acts when we consider that Christianity has maintained for two thousand years that the Jews killed God incarnate. Only when Pius's illustrious and righteous successor, John XXIII, convened Vatican II were Jews finally absolved of the charges of deicide.

Without condoning or excusing such behavior, we can easily imagine how an allegation of such severity might make some Christians indifferent to Jewish suffering. For this reason, we must now put to final rest the utter falsity of the idea that Jews killed Jesus and that Jesus hated his own people.

Part II

The Death of Jesus

CHAPTER 10

THE CRUCIFIXION

The story of Jesus' crucifixion is one of the best-known stories in human history. Even the most casual New Testament reader is familiar with the general outline: Jesus was betrayed by his follower Judas, extended clemency by Pontius Pilate, but then denounced by the Pharisees and Jewish onlookers, after which he was nailed to a cross, dying on what would come to be known as Good Friday.

Yet, if we've learned anything from our study of Jesus' life, it's that there is often more to it than meets the eye. Embedded in the various Gospel versions of this well-worn story are a number of substantive contradictions that call into question the very fundamentals of its retelling. In these disagreements we get a clear view of the machinations of New Testament editors as they found it necessary to rewrite history.

The first three Gospels – Matthew, Mark, and Luke – all focus on Jesus' victimhood at the hands of Jews and Romans. Yet in the Book of John, the story is reversed.

The last of the Gospels to be written, John tells an almost unrecognizably different story. Jesus actually volunteers to lay down his life. In complete control of the situation, Jesus says to people, including Pontius Pilate, that the only reason the Romans can put him to death is because *he himself wills it*. John even gives the impression that Jesus experiences no pain. From the outset, he is a lamb that goes to the slaughter willingly and does not suffer.

This could not be more in conflict with the account given by Matthew, in which Jesus suffers terribly on the cross. He cries out, "My God, my God, why have you forsaken me?"[101] These are words of unspeakable anguish and abandonment – certainly not words that would be spoken by someone willingly submitting to torture and death.

The other two Gospels portray the horror and misery of this event in unstinting detail. Mark describes a scene in which Jesus is mocked and brutalized by Roman soldiers: "The soldiers led Jesus into the palace.... They put a purple robe on him, then twisted together a crown of thorns and set it on him. And they began to call out to him, 'Hail, king of the Jews!' Again and again they struck him on the head with a staff and spit on him. Falling on their knees, they paid homage to him. And when they had mocked him, they took off the purple robe and put his own clothes on him. Then they led him out to crucify him."[102] Luke paints a picture of Jesus crucified alongside two criminals, as onlookers taunted: "The people stood watching, and the rulers even sneered at him. They said, 'He saved others; let him save himself if he is God's Messiah, the Chosen One.'"[103]

The obvious question that arises is, simply, *what changed*? How did the Gospels contort Jesus' crucifixion from the pathos of Mark, Matthew, and Luke to the strange detachment described by John?

It seems clear that this was a rewriting calculated to appeal to Roman readers after Jesus' death. The culture of Rome thrived on power and masculine virility. The Roman people would never have been impressed with a weak Jesus, as he was described in the first three Gospels. Though the idea of victimhood and martyrdom would have appealed to Jews who were themselves victims of Roman brutality, the Romans could never relate to a deity that gets beaten up and crucified by centurions. They were the strongest people on earth! They revered aggression, not weakness. Any deity pathetic enough to be put to death by low-ranking Roman soldiers could not be a deity at all.

The editor of the Book of John, last of the Gospels, faces a quandary. He cannot change the facts. They have already been reported in historical accounts and other Gospels. Jesus had been crucified by the Romans – case closed. But since he must do *something* to rescue Jesus' virility, he changes the mechanics and motivations of the story. The most important verse in all of John, so crucial that we shall devote later chapters to understanding its ramifications, should be familiar to all Christians: "For God so loved the world that he gave his one and only Son, that whoever believes in him shall not perish but have eternal life."[104] John envisages Jesus as an all-powerful deity who willingly laid down his life to atone for the sins of mankind. Hence, Jesus barely suffers throughout the Passion. It is all part of a divine plan.

This isn't the only discrepancy that John introduces. Six hundred Roman soldiers come to arrest Jesus but end up bowing at his feet. Not only that, he receives a royal burial.[105] Jesus even exhibits awareness of his predestined fate when he tells Pilate, "You would have no power over me if it were not given to you from above."[106] How different this is from the other three Gospels.

The many significant discrepancies in the crucifixion story suggest alterations by multiple editors and authors. These disagreements include the fact that Mark has three women going to anoint the body of Jesus after the crucifixion. As he tells it, "When the Sabbath was over, Mary Magdalene, Mary the mother of James, and Salome bought spices so that they might go to anoint Jesus' body. Very early on the first day of the week, just after sunrise, they were on their way to the tomb and they asked each other, 'Who will roll the stone away from the entrance of the tomb?' But when they looked up, they saw that the stone, which was very large, had been rolled away."[107] Yet Matthew says only two women went: "After the Sabbath, at dawn on the first day of the week, Mary Magdalene and the other Mary went to look at the tomb."[108] Note they were only going to see the tomb, not to anoint Jesus. In John's telling, the number of visitor changes yet again. "Early on the first day of the week, while it was still dark, Mary Magdalene went to the tomb and saw that the stone had been removed from the entrance."[109]

Something doesn't quite add up.

We all know the Romans hated the early Christians. In his palace, the Roman emperor Nero burned Christians alive for amusement. The Romans fed Christians to lions as a form of entertainment at the Colosseum. So why should we believe the New Testament's assertion that the Jews tried to kill Jesus and his disciples while the Romans admired them?

We cannot accept this version – the crude picture of evil Jews plotting the death of one of their own, nor the propagandistic description of the impotent Romans innocent of the brutality meted out on the central figure of Christianity.

Indeed, the discrepancies between the Passion narratives and the lack of historical evidence have led many prominent scholars of the Christian Bible and its history to conclude decisively that these narratives were later additions – adaptations made to redefine Christianity and help it survive in new, changing political and social circumstances.

PETER ACCUSES THE JEWS

Further proof of this concerted effort to exonerate the Romans and implicate the Jews in the death of Jesus comes from the Gospel of Peter. Though it was ultimately declared apocryphal and left out of the biblical canon, Peter's story was very influential during Christianity's formative years.

A profoundly anti-Semitic document, this Gospel was written by the same Peter who denied knowing Jesus three times when confronted by the Romans. Amazingly, Peter claims it was the Jews who crucified Christ – the Jews not only handed Jesus over to the Romans, they actually *carried out the crucifixion.*

According to Peter's uncanonized gospel, the Romans and Pontius Pilate withdrew completely from the trial of Jesus, leaving Herod Antipas and the Jews themselves to crucify him. "But of the Jews none washed their hands, neither Herod nor any of his judges. And as they would not wash, Pilate arose. And then Herod the king commanded that the Lord should be marched off, saying to them, 'What I have commanded you to do him, do ye,'... And he delivered him to the people on the day before the unleavened bread, their feast."[110]

Elsewhere, in the Book of Acts, Peter twice accuses the Jews of having killed Jesus. He makes no mention of the Romans when he denounces the Jews, saying, "Therefore let all Israel be assured of this: God has made this Jesus, whom you crucified, both Lord and Messiah."[111] Later Peter tells members of the Jewish council: "The God of our ancestors raised Jesus from the dead – whom you killed by hanging him on a cross."[112]

Only once does he deign to mention the involvement of the Romans. Even when he does, he takes pains to inoculate Pontius Pilate from criticism: "The God of Abraham, Isaac, and Jacob, the God of our fathers, has glorified his servant Jesus. You handed him over to be killed, and you disowned him before Pilate, *though he had decided to let him go.*"[113]

Can we believe Peter when he claims the Jews killed Jesus or at the very least handed him over to the Romans? Should we take as gospel his abject whitewashing of the behavior of Pontius Pilate? No, absolutely not.

Peter's allegedly eyewitness testimony contains many problems. At the top of the list is the fact that Jesus himself accused Peter of being a liar. Jesus told Peter the night before he died, in one of the best-known stories of the New Testament, that before the next morning Peter would deny him three times: "Jesus told them, 'This very night you will all fall away on account of me,'... Peter replied, 'Even if all fall away on account of you, I never will.' 'Truly I tell you,' Jesus answered, 'this very night, before the rooster crows, you will disown me three times.'"[114] Just as Jesus predicts, when a servant girl approaches him and asserts that he was among Jesus' followers, Peter says, "I don't know what you're talking about."[115] She accuses him again before a crowd, and he denies it again. It even happens a third time: "After a little while, those standing there went up to Peter and said, 'Surely you are one of them; your accent gives you away.' Then he began to call down curses, and he swore to them, 'I don't know the man!'"[116] Peter denies Jesus in order to save his own skin, leaving his master to be murdered.

Jesus' serious misgivings about Peter's character are already in evidence in his prediction that Peter will turn out to be a liar. Peter's abandonment of Jesus at his most desperate moment in order to save himself is even more troubling, especially given that Peter would eventually succeed to the leadership of the Church. It seems impossible that a brazen coward, whom Jesus himself knew would lie about their relationship, would be taken seriously when he later accuses the Jews of having killed Jesus. We know that, according to Jesus, Peter would say anything to save himself. And if that entails appeasing the Romans by selling out the Jews as well, we shouldn't be surprised that Peter is prepared to do that, too.

Peter seems to be trying to use the Jews as a scapegoat for his own failure to protect his master. He knows he should have stood by Jesus. But rather than take responsibility for his betrayal, he blames someone else. His moral failures certainly cast doubt on anything he says about Jewish involvement in the murder of Jesus.

Like Jesus, the Jews were fearless in the face of almost certain death at the hands of their cruel Roman overlords. Respected Jews like Jesus and the other Pharisaic rabbis were known for their courage in confronting the Romans. The Talmud is replete with stories of great Jewish sages tortured by the Romans in the most horrific ways because of their opposition to the emperor's brutal rule. But Peter watches the Romans arrest his teacher, and not only does he not protest, he actually denies even knowing him. Humiliated, he chooses to shift the blame and indict those who were so much more courageous in order to exonerate himself.

Importantly, Peter's testimony of the Jews actually killing Jesus directly contradicts the New Testament. As we've seen, all four Gospels are adamant that, whatever role the Gospels insist the Jews played in agitating for Jesus' death, it was most certainly the Romans who actually crucified him.

Indeed, the New Testament goes so far as to tell us explicitly that not only did the Pharisees not kill Jesus, they actually tried to save his life. At the very beginning of Jesus' preaching, when Herod wants to kill him for sedition, the rabbis inform Jesus of the threat to his life and order him to flee: "At that time some Pharisees came to Jesus and said to him, 'Leave this place and go somewhere else. Herod wants to kill you.'"[117] Only by willfully ignoring the established facts about Jesus' death could Peter have come up with his anti-Semitic falsehoods.

CHAPTER 11

DID JUDAS REALLY EXIST?

As Peter's brand of anti-Semitism gathered force over the years, Judas Iscariot became a favorite figure for Christian thinkers and writers intent on castigating the Jews. A perfect villain, the former apostle was willing to sell his teacher out for a couple of gold coins. To many anti-Semitic Christians, he seemed the very model of the money-grubbing, perfidious Jew – and for that, they made him famous.

These thinkers found it easy to smear the Jews by pointing to the dichotomy of the figures of Peter and Judas. Peter was a representative of the Church, while Judas stood in for the Jews. Augustine of Hippo set the stage for centuries of anti-Jewish feeling by writing, "One wicked man [Judas] represents the whole body of the wicked; in the same way as Peter, the whole body of the good, yea, the body of the Church."[118] Similarly, Saint Jerome (374–419 CE) used Judas to associate Jews with the treacherous serpent in the Garden of Eden, denouncing Jews as "Judaic serpents of whom Judas was the model."

In dramatic literature and art, Judas embodies the anti-Jewish polemic. Artists usually endow Judas with grossly exaggerated Semitic features, such as a giant nose, and he is often grubby and dirty. His love for money and readiness to sell out his most vital interests for cash serve as a model for several other anti-Semitic caricatures, most notably Shakespeare's miserly Shylock. No wonder Christian thinkers have traditionally made Judas as devilish as possible. As early as the fourth century, Pope Gelasius I summed up how many

Christians still view Judas: "In the Bible, the whole is often named after the part: as Judas was called a devil and the devil's workman, he gives his name to the whole race."[119]

It's not hard to see where this idea originated. In the New Testament itself, Judas is frequently shown as a conduit of Satan. In the Book of Luke, it is casually stated, "Then Satan entered Judas, called Iscariot."[120] In another variation on that same idea, the Book of John notes, "As soon as Judas took the bread, Satan entered into him."[121] Before the Last Supper, John even informs us, "The devil had already prompted Judas, the son of Simon Iscariot, to betray Jesus."[122]

Alone among the other Gospels, the Book of John goes a step further, stitching Judas' obsession with money into the story. In the Gospel of John, Judas is the treasurer of Jesus' organization and embezzles from the common funds. According to one story, "Then Mary took about a pint of pure nard, an expensive perfume; she poured it on Jesus' feet and wiped his feet with her hair. And the house was filled with the fragrance of the perfume. But one of his disciples, Judas Iscariot, who was later to betray him, objected, 'Why wasn't this perfume sold and the money given to the poor? It was worth a year's wages.'"[123] Naturally, Judas does not say this because he cares about the poor. In John's eyes, he is a thief. As keeper of the purse, he has already been seen helping himself to its contents, and he wants to make sure he won't miss a single coin.

Even isolated as it is in the Gospel of John, this portrayal of Judas' supposedly acquisitive ways had real and lasting consequences for the Jewish community. For, as Hyam Maccoby has observed, "The association of Christian society to drive the Jews into money-lending as their sole permitted occupation, owes much to this emblematic portrayal of Judas."[124]

It is already suspicious that this story occurs in only one out of four Gospels. And other signs of editorial meddling are immediately in evidence. As Maccoby demonstrates, this story seems to be a simple amalgamation of two earlier stories found elsewhere. "The first (Mark 14:3–9; Matthew 26:6–11; Luke 7:37) also takes place in Bethany. An unnamed woman pours precious ointment on Jesus' head, and is reproved – not by Judas Iscariot, but by 'some of the present' (Mark) or by the 'disciples' (Matthew) – for wasting ointment that could have been sold to benefit the poor.... The second story (Luke 10:38–42) concerns the two sisters Martha and Mary, but it is situated only in 'a certain village,' not Bethany, nor does it refer to precious ointment."[125] It seems clear that this tale of Judas' corruption, so vital to smearing all Jews as money-grubbers, is a fabrication, and one that falls apart after the merest scrutiny.

Today, most Christians remember Judas as the betrayer of Jesus. Here is John's retelling of that event:

> When he had finished praying, Jesus left with his disciples and crossed the Kidron Valley. On the other side there was a garden, and he and his disciples went into it. Now Judas, who betrayed him, knew the place, because Jesus had often met there with his disciples. So Judas came to the garden, guiding a detachment of soldiers and some officials from the chief priests and the Pharisees. They were carrying torches, lanterns and weapons. Jesus, knowing all that was going to happen to him, went out and asked them, "Who is it you want?"
>
> "Jesus of Nazareth," they replied.
>
> "I am he," Jesus said. (And Judas the traitor was standing there with them.)[126]

After that, we hear nothing further of Judas. As far as John's Gospel is concerned, Judas has proven himself evil incarnate. Having betrayed Jesus, he loses his identity and is no longer of interest. But there is something startling in this story if only we look closer.

Only in this fragment of John does the true story come out. Jesus, a rebellious Jew, has been arrested by Roman troops. They arrested him with the assistance of Jewish collaborators, Judas among them, intent on betraying the leader of the Jewish resistance to the Roman occupation. What makes the story so remarkable is that everywhere else, the Book of John takes great pains to demonstrate that Jesus had no political mission whatsoever. So why does the real story suddenly emerge here of all places? Incomplete and careless editing has allowed a sliver of the undeniable truth to remain: Jesus was arrested not by henchmen of the high priests but by Roman troops, enforcers against sedition.

JUDAS THE SYMBOLIC FIGURE

Many scholars now believe Judas Iscariot never existed in the first place, and was written into the story solely to incriminate the Jews. Among others, leading Christian scholar Raymond Brown matter-of-factly writes in *The Death of the Messiah* that many scholars believe that Judas never existed but was a symbolic figure.[127]

The first and most compelling reason to think so is the simple fact of Judas' name. That the apostle whose very name literally means "Jew" is the one to turn in Jesus seems contrived in the extreme.

Also, if Judas did exist, it is shocking that Paul never mentions him throughout all of his works. Paul revels in the death of Jesus, modeling his entire spiritual-philosophical system after the events of the crucifixion. If a man named Judas were involved, he would have certainly used such a story in his proselytizing. Yet he does not even mention the apostle who allegedly betrayed Jesus above all others. This glaring omission seems utterly baffling until we consider that Paul's epistles were written before the Gospels. It seems very plausible that the story of Judas took root only after Paul's death. He gives it absolutely no mention because Judas hasn't yet been invented.

Giving further credence to this concept are the number of early Gospel iterations in which Judas is missing, despite being present in later Gospel versions. These scenes, too, bear clear marks of substantial rewriting.

Peter's uncanonized gospel refers to the presence of twelve apostles even after Jesus' death. "Now it was the last day of the unleavened bread, and many were going forth, returning to their homes, as the feast was ended. But we, *the twelve disciples of the Lord*, wept and were grieved; and each one, being grieved for that which was come to pass, departed to his home."[128] Hyam Maccoby has pointed out that whoever wrote the Gospel of Peter must have been unaware that Judas supposedly had already left Jesus' inner circle, according to accounts in the accepted Gospels. This discrepancy also supports the idea that the entire character of Judas was a fabrication.[129]

Yet among the most convincing indications that Judas was fictional is his biblical precursor. Most Christian readers will be unaware of the Hebrew Bible story of Ahitophel, King David's treacherous adviser. Yet the similarities between Ahitophel and Judas are glaringly conspicuous. These shared elements point to a deliberate attempt to make Jesus look like David, the first messianic king, and to cast the Jews as traitors responsible for the murder of Jesus.

Both Ahitophel and Judas are traitors, leading armies to the man they are betraying. The Second Book of Samuel describes the scene. Ahitophel says to Absalom, David's son, who has rebelled and usurped the throne and seeks his father's life: "I would choose twelve thousand men and set out tonight in pursuit of David. I would attack him while he is weary and weak. I would strike him with terror, and then all the people with him will flee. I would strike down only the king and bring all the people back to you. The death of the man you seek will mean the return of all; all the people will be unharmed."[130]

If we compare this passage to the story of Judas as related in the Gospel of Mark, parallels swiftly become apparent: "Just as he was speaking, Judas, one of the Twelve, appeared. With him was a crowd armed with swords and clubs, sent from the chief priests, the teachers of the law, and the elders. Now the betrayer had arranged a signal with them: 'The one I kiss is the man; arrest him and lead him away under guard.' Going at once to Jesus, Judas said, 'Rabbi!' and kissed him."[131] Ahitophel and Judas, betrayers of Jewish kings for personal interest, seem cut from the same cloth.

Judas and Ahitophel are also drawn together by the fact that both commit suicide. The Hebrew Bible describes the scene: "When Ahithophel saw that his advice had not been followed, he saddled his donkey and set out for his house in his hometown. He put his house in order and then hanged himself. So he died and was buried in his father's tomb."[132] Judas does the same: "When Judas, who had betrayed him, saw that Jesus was condemned, he was seized with remorse and returned the thirty silver coins to the chief priests and the elders.... So Judas threw the money into the temple and left. Then he went away and hanged himself."[133]

To sum up, Ahitophel and Judas are both treacherous disciples who lead armies to capture their former masters and commit suicide by hanging themselves.

Indeed, the story of Judas kissing Jesus in an act of betrayal seems reminiscent of an earlier biblical story as well. As Maccoby writes:

> It has been suggested that the story was influenced by the Hebrew Bible story of Joab and Amasa, the two rival generals of King David. Joab falls into disfavor with the king, and was replaced as commander-in-chief by Amasa. But when he was charged with leading reinforcement troops to help Amasa, Joab treacherously contrived to assassinate him. "And Joab

said to Amasa, 'Is it well with thee, my brother?' And Joab took Amasa by the beard with his right hand to kiss him.'"

The image of betrayal by a kiss is undoubtedly there in both stories, and it is clearly a story-motif common in the East. It is expressed also in the Hebrew Bible in the form of a proverb: "The blows of a friend are well-meant, but the kisses of an enemy are perfidious." (Proverbs 27:6)[134]

With each detail it seems ever more clear that, between his textual forebears and his transparently concocted name, Judas is none other than a literary creation.

But the greatest piece of evidence for the nonexistence of Judas is the fact that the New Testament later gives a completely different story of how Judas died. The story quoted above, describing Judas' hanging, is directly contradicted by the Book of Acts, in which Judas dies due to a horrible divine punishment:

> In those days Peter stood up among the believers (a group numbering about a hundred and twenty) and said, "Brothers, the Scripture had to be fulfilled in which the Holy Spirit spoke long ago through David concerning Judas, who served as guide for those who arrested Jesus. He was one of our number and shared in our ministry." (With the payment he received for his wickedness, Judas bought a field; there he fell headlong, his body burst open, and all his intestines spilled out. Everyone in Jerusalem heard about this, so they called that field in their language Akeldama, that is, Field of Blood.)[135]

This death mimics the prescribed biblical death for a *sotah*, an unfaithful wife. When she drinks the holy waters of the Temple, into which the priests have scraped the name of God, her belly bloats, her thigh wilts, and she inflates until she bursts.[136] The authors of the

New Testament wanted to show that Judas, as an unfaithful disciple, received the same punishment for his faithlessness. The two tales of the death of Judas are irreconcilable, indicating that, in all probability, neither is accurate.

Paipas, the Bishop of Hierapolis about a hundred years after Jesus' death, tried to reconcile both stories, claiming that Judas failed in his attempt to hang himself and lived for a while as an example of what happens to those who defy Jesus.

> As a great example of impiety, Judas walked about in this world. He was so swollen in his body, that there where a wagon could go through easily, he could not go through; nay, he could not even insert the mass of his head. His eyelids were so swollen, it is said, that he could not see the light at all, nor could his eyes be seen even with an optical instrument; so deep did they lie from the surface.
>
> His genitals were repellent and huge beyond all shamelessness. From his whole body flowed blood mixed with worms, which exuded particularly during his natural needs.
>
> After many trials and sufferings, they say, he died in his own place, which, because of the stench, has remained deserted and uninhabitable to the present day. Until today, no one can pass by that place without holding his nose. So great was the exudation from his body that spread over the ground.[137]

Judas thus became the first Jew to survive in the Augustinian model as an example to the rest of the world.

Yet even so, virtually every detail about Judas' story indicates it was devised after Jesus' death and developed into a tool for using anti-Semitism to define and promote Christianity. Even the notion that the Romans would need the help of a traitor from Jesus' disciples seems to contradict the New Testament's repeated assertions that Jesus was welcomed into Jerusalem with giant throngs of people awaiting his entry. Clearly, Jesus was an extremely well-known figure whom the Romans, and their Jewish priest collaborators, could easily identify without assistance.

Yet even these transparent fictionalizations pale in comparison to the whitewashing of Pontius Pilate's character, as we shall soon see.

CHAPTER 12

BRUTAL PILATE

Almost as offensive as Peter's claim that the Jews crucified Jesus was the claim, still widely accepted, that Pontius Pilate was innocent of any crime. As previously explained, in the anti-Semitic environment following the Great Revolt of 70 CE, the latter-day editors of the New Testament needed to sanitize the story of Jesus' crucifixion and shift all traces of villainy away from the Romans. These efforts led them to concoct the transparent falsehood that Pilate was anything less than a brutal murderer.

The Gospel of Matthew describes the alleged confrontation between Pilate and the Jews:

> "What shall I do, then, with Jesus who is called the Messiah?" Pilate asked. They all answered, "Crucify him!" "Why? What crime has he committed?" asked Pilate. But they shouted all the louder, "Crucify him!" When Pilate saw that he was getting nowhere, but that instead an uproar was starting, he took water and washed his hands in front of the crowd. "I am innocent of this man's blood," he said. "It is your responsibility!" All the people answered, "His blood is on us and on our children!"[138]

Throughout history, this sequence – this very paragraph – has been used time and again to justify the worst Christian atrocities against Jews. It remains a crucial point of contention between the two religions even today. Yet most scholars who investigate the details of both the historical record and the New Testament accounts agree from the evidence that this exchange is not just implausible but outright impossible.

The Book of Matthew indicates that just five days earlier the Jews gave Jesus a very enthusiastic welcome to Jerusalem. "A very large crowd [was present, who] spread their cloaks on the road, while others cut branches from the trees and spread them on the road. The crowds that went ahead of him and those that followed shouted, 'Hosanna to the Son of David!' 'Blessed is he who comes in the name of the Lord!' 'Hosanna in the highest heaven!'"[139]

If we take the Gospels at face value, this hero's welcome transforms into a throng of Jews commiserating with a Roman proconsul – whom, let us not forget, they hated and who hated them. The public is supposed to have turned against Jesus exceedingly quickly, going from lionizing him as a conquering prophet to demanding his immediate execution within a week's time.

In fact, the exchange between Pilate and the Jews bears obvious signs of fictionalizing. Pilate had no need to answer to the people and no desire to be beholden to anyone not in the Roman organizational hierarchy. He cared little about due process or justice. He was a tyrant who represented the deadly authoritarianism from which the Jews sought relief. The story that Pilate would seek or follow the wishes of the non-Romans he despised emerged only as a brazen *post hoc* attempt to implicate the Jews in the murder of Jesus and exonerate the true murderers.

The presentation in the New Testament of Pilate as a humanitarian Führer with a benevolent heart makes for a public relations fiction worthy of Joseph Göbbels. The truth is that Pilate was nothing less than the Hitler of his time, a brutal and bloodthirsty monster who routinely murdered thousands of innocents without trial. Leading historians of the time all agree Pilate was a sadistic mass murderer who reveled in his autocratic powers. He was so cruel, Emperor

Tiberius was forced to recall him from the governor's post in 36 CE. Imagine how violent one must be to merit being removed from a foreign post by the Romans!

Yet is was so; even Pilate's Roman peers despised him. King Herod Agrippa I wrote a letter to Caligula, who had become emperor in 37 CE, reminding him of Pilate's by-now dismissed acts of violence, "his corruption, and his acts of insolence, and his rapine, and his habit of insulting people, and his cruelty, and his continual murders of persons untried and uncondemned, and his never-ending, and gratuitous, and most grievous inhumanity." A contemporary of Pilate, the great Jewish philosopher Philo considered the Roman governor to be "a man of a very inflexible disposition, and very merciless as well as very obstinate."[140]

Pilate had begun his career as procurator by attempting to bring a statue of Caesar into Judea. He knew this would be anathema to the Jews. The emperor was, after all, worshipped as a living god, something the monotheistic Jews could never abide. Pilate continued to stir up disturbances, during which many Jews were killed. In *Antiquities*, Josephus relates that Pilate's excessive murders and sadistic brutality later got him recalled to Rome, in the year 36 CE, following his slaughter of four thousand supporters of a Samaritan prophet.[141]

Even Rome's most well-known historian, Cornelius Tacitus, admitted to Pilate's culpability. About the crucifixion of Jesus, he wrote, "Christus, the founder of the name, had undergone the death penalty in the reign of Tiberius, by sentence of the procurator Pontius Pilate, and the pernicious superstition was checked for the moment, only to break out once more, not merely in Judea, the home of the disease, but in the capital itself, where all things horrible or shameful in the world collect and find a vogue."[142] Tacitus had nothing but contempt for Christianity and for Jesus himself. Any report on the Jews dealing treacherously with one of their own would have delighted him to no end. However, such a claim had yet to be fabricated, and he pinned blame squarely on Pilate, precisely where it belongs.

Historian Gregory Baum sums up the real Pontius Pilate as being incomparably violent and malicious. "Pilate," he says, "was certainly the worst of the Roman procurators of Judea. How can this Pilate, of whom Luke reports that he contrived a massacre of Galileans worshipping in the temple, suddenly turn into a soft, hesitating, and justice-loving man who needs the approval of the crowd to come to a decision?"[143] And given that men of unimaginable brutality regularly held the governor's post, calling Pilate the worst of the lot makes for quite a potent condemnation.

Those Christian readers who may deny my assessment of Pilate need look only at what Jesus said on the subject. In the Book of Luke, Jesus himself evokes Pilate's inhumanity perhaps most eloquently of all. At one point, Pilate massacres a huge group of Galileans worshipping in the Temple. "Now there were some present at that time who told Jesus about the Galileans whose blood Pilate had mixed with their sacrifices. Jesus answered, 'Do you think that these Galileans were worse sinners than all the other Galileans because they suffered this way? I tell you, no! But unless you repent, you too will all perish.'"[144]

This is a fascinating passage. Jesus here uses Pilate as a living warning to his disciples, explaining that the monstrous Pilate does not care whether they are righteous or not. Jesus tells his students that the barbarous Pilate will murder them and mix their blood with that of the animal sacrifices – an obscenely brutal and disgusting act – unless they repent. Therefore, they should choose righteousness and gird themselves to oppose the idolaters ruling over them.

Luke's Pilate, indiscriminately mixing Jewish blood with the blood of the holy sacrifices, is the same one Matthew portrays as a "softie," reluctant to execute another Galilean. The editors of the

Book of Matthew still take pains to show Pilate attempting to save Jesus' life by briefly opposing the will of the Jewish mob. Clearly, the Matthew text results from deliberate spin-doctoring – an effort conducted by New Testament editors, well after the death of Jesus, to slander the Jews and separate Judaism from Jesus. These editors also sought to rehabilitate Pilate, transforming him from a bloodthirsty tyrant into the unwitting agent of Jewish passion – a convenient and utter falsehood.

CHAPTER 13

BARABBAS

The New Testament relates that when Jesus was crucified, a Jewish convict named Barabbas went with him. From all four Gospels, we learn that Barabbas took part in some kind of rebellion against Rome. For that reason, when Pilate gives the Jews an opportunity to release one prisoner, the Jews call for Barabbas' release.[145] As Mark tells the story:

> Now it was the custom at the festival to release a prisoner whom the people requested. A man called Barabbas was in prison with the insurrectionists who had committed murder in the uprising. The crowd came up and asked Pilate to do for them what he usually did. "Do you want me to release to you the king of the Jews?" asked Pilate, knowing it was out of self-interest that the chief priests had handed Jesus over to him. But the chief priests stirred up the crowd to have Pilate release Barabbas instead.[146]

On the very face of it, this story has ample problems. For one thing, the Romans never had any such practice of releasing murderers and rebels on the people's whim. Not even on a holiday like Passover did this happen. If it were true, nearly any rebel against Roman authority, or for that matter any sociopathic killer, could be released if only the crowd bayed loudly enough. Such a practice would make a mockery of Roman law and order. Sure enough, Philo of Alexandria explains that on the holiday of an occupied people, the practice was

86

altogether different. Rather than releasing a prisoner, the Romans would delay execution.[147] Pilate would never have released a murderer like Barabbas just to make the Jews happy, although he might have held up his execution until after Passover.

Furthermore, Barabbas' appearance in the narrative seems staged and unbelievable. Why would such a beloved character show up so late in the narrative? If Barabbas was so adored by the masses, would he not have received a triumphal entry to Jerusalem similar to the one Jesus received? There is something odd about the Barabbas tale from the very beginning.

Among other critics, biblical scholar John Crossan maintains Barabbas probably never existed and was instead written into the New Testament to serve as a metaphor. The architects of the New Testament were saying that when the Jews had a chance to choose between a man of peace, Jesus, and a brigand who wanted rebellion, they opted to free the brigand. They saved the rebel against Rome, while the peaceful Jesus, who had promoted a spiritual revolution, was put to death. Early Christian authors probably invented this character to further emphasize that Jesus never challenged Roman authority the way Barabbas did.

Hyam Maccoby goes even further, hypothesizing the story of Barabbas is actually a remnant of Jesus' own true story. After all, the story of Barabbas in the New Testament seems to align with the vision of Jesus as we saw it in the first chapter of this book. He was a Jewish rebel against Rome beloved by the Jewish people for his devotion to them. This is a fascinating interpretation on the part of Maccoby. He believes Barabbas is the Jesus whose political rebellion against Rome incurred the wrath of the legions and who was therefore sentenced to death by crucifixion, while the Jesus who is crucified for his rebellion against Judaism is the product of the Christian retelling of an embellished story.

Whether Barabbas was kept in the story because his is the real story of Jesus or not, Jews certainly had no control over who lived or died. The Romans never granted them that kind of power. The Jews remained an occupied people with no other power than to obey.[148]

CHAPTER 14

A POLITICAL DEATH AND
THE TRIAL OF JESUS

We've seen that the Gospels were heavily edited, such that Pontius Pilate was posthumously exonerated in spite of his vile brutality. Already, one can reasonably conclude the Romans bear more responsibility for Jesus' death than Christians may have previously thought. Now, let's examine Jesus' execution itself.

What better proof can we find of Jesus' true nature as a politician and Jewish patriot than the manner of his death? If he were put to death for blasphemy, he would not have been crucified. Jesus was killed by the distinctly Roman form of capital punishment reserved for political rebels against the rule of Rome: crucifixion on a cross.

Crucifixion is one of the most horrible forms of capital punishment ever devised. It was a method of torture and execution the Romans had adopted from their former enemies, the Carthaginians. The victim is fastened to an upright scaffold and left dangling. Gravity forces blood away from the heart while the spread-eagle position permits only shallow breathing. Roman victims were often scourged first so that their flesh hung in ribbons. Death, caused by asphyxiation and exhaustion, could take up to three excruciating days.

Death on the cross was a punishment usually reserved for rebellious slaves, but in a conquered territory such as Palestine, Roman officials used it to punish acts of insurrection or rebellion against their occupation. The fact that Jesus died on the cross further testifies to his position as a Jewish rebel leader.

This point cannot be overstated. Crucifixion was the Romans' most brutal form of death, the near-certain fate for any political rebel. If Jesus were a religious opponent of the rabbis as the Gospels allege, he would never have been crucified. In fact, there is nothing Jesus did that would have ever warranted death at the hands of the rabbis, as we'll soon explore. So why, then, do the Gospels tell us the Jews gave Jesus a death sentence?

Jesus' trial by the Sanhedrin, the Jewish Supreme Court, is a fundamental thread in the New Testament's larger argument that the Jews killed Jesus because he sought to undermine Judaism and the Law. We are told that Jesus was a rebel – not against Rome, but against the Jewish religion. Therefore the great rabbis gathered together to indict him and condemn him to death. The problem is there is almost certainly no truth to the account of the trial.

We are told that the Sanhedrin, consisting of the seventy-one greatest sages in Israel, condemned Jesus to death. Yet there are suspicious rewritings evident in the descriptions of the trial. In the Gospel of Mark we read that members of the Sanhedrin like Joseph of Arimathea, "a prominent member of the Council," risked everything to ask Pilate that Jesus' body be removed from the cross.[149] Taken at face value, this detail shows that even in the Sanhedrin Jesus had many supporters. It is only reasonable to ask: If Joseph of Arimathea were such an influential member of the Sanhedrin, wouldn't he have approached Pilate and objected to the crucifixion from the beginning? Where were he and the rest of the supporters when this court allegedly sentenced Jesus to such a cruel death?

Sure enough, the Book of Matthew accounts for this incongruity. The author recognizes that if Joseph of Arimathea were a member of the Sanhedrin, he could have intervened to save Jesus. To smooth over this detail, Matthew simply changes the story, stripping Joseph of his membership in the Sanhedrin altogether. He claims that while

Joseph is a rich man, he is not of the Sanhedrin.[150] Problem solved, though evidence of editorial rewriting of the facts remains.

Other inconsistencies abound. According to the Gospels of Mark, Matthew, and Luke, the trial of Jesus took place the first night of Passover at the seder. The Last Supper must therefore have been a seder meal. If so, Jesus must have eaten matzo and wine, the principal foods of the seder table. Yet the Gospel of John contradicts this, saying the trial of Jesus took place not on the first night of Passover but the second.

This is quite a discrepancy. In Jesus' time the first night of Passover was the only night a seder was held. It was also the only evening where the paschal lamb was brought to the Temple and eaten. To mix up dates as significant as these would have been improbable for Jesus' followers. It is far more likely that the story is a later invention by zealous New Testament editors.

Even if the Gospels were correct about the trial of Jesus, however, the unlikeliest element of all is the suggestion that the Sanhedrin met at night, and on the first night of Passover no less. This would have violated all of the court's rules. The Sanhedrin was the highest Jewish court, and its meetings were not taken lightly. Like American courts, the Sanhedrin never met on holidays or in the evening. The Talmud records a law that expressly forbade the Sanhedrin to pass judgment by night.[151] Maimonides codified this law as well. The ancient rabbis were concerned that if courts met at night, the justices would be tired and consequently rush through cases to get home, thereby corrupting justice. For the same reason, there were absolutely no capital judgments on the eve of any festival.[152] The ideals of justice and mercy were foremost in the minds of the Sanhedrin, and theirs was a truly awesome responsibility in Israel.

For the Sanhedrin to convene during off-hours to deal with an unknown rebel like Jesus, whose crime was, according to the New Testament, nothing more than blasphemy, is unlikely in the extreme. It would be as implausible as the United States Supreme Court agreeing on short notice to meet on Christmas Eve because a young trouble-maker had burned an American flag outside the Washington Monument. Would Supreme Court justices leave their families to quickly condemn such an alleged offender to death? I don't think so.

Now some might say, okay, these were the rules. But maybe these judges were so afraid of Jesus' challenge to religious sensibilities that they agreed to set aside all the rules. Come what may, they were going to act swiftly to put Jesus to death. This argument is equally without merit. Jews with such a lack of respect for Jewish law as to conduct a trial on the first night of Passover and quickly condemn an innocent man to death are equally unlikely to have been concerned about any transgression of Jewish law by Jesus, or to be chosen for service on the nation's board of highest legal authority.

The text of the New Testament gives us many additional reasons to conclude that the rabbinic trial of Jesus never took place. Paul never once mentions the trial of Jesus, and the accounts in the first two Gospels are highly tendentious, severely conflicting with one another.

There are no fewer than three different and contradictory versions of the trial of Jesus. According to the Gospel of John, one and a half trials took place. Mark and Matthew tell us there were actually two trials, while Luke goes so far as to relate three separate trials. In his movie *The Passion of the Christ*, Mel Gibson chose to portray the Lucan version where, first, the Jewish priests put Jesus on trial. Then, Herod Antipas gave him another separate trial. Finally, Pontius Pilate met with Jesus to try him once again. Luke goes out of his way to condemn the Jews much more seriously than the other Gospels. In Luke, Herod and Pilate actually agree to let Jesus go and give him fancy robes to wear. The Jews alone bray for his blood, according to Luke (and later, Mel Gibson).

According to scholars of early Christianity such as John Dominic Crossan, no trial ever took place.

> The trial is, in my best judgment, based entirely on prophecy historicized rather than history remembered. It is not just the content of the trial but the very fact of the trial that I consider to be unhistorical.... Imagine that Caiaphas and Pilate had standing agreements and orders concerning Passover, whereby any subversive action involving the Temple and its crowds would beget instant punishment with immediate crucifixion as public warning and deterrent. There would be no need to go very high up the chain of command for a peasant nuisance nobody like Jesus, no need for even a formal interrogation before Caiaphas, let alone a detailed trial before Pilate. In the case of Jesus, there may well have been Arrest and Execution but no trial whatsoever in between.[153]

We are forced to accept that history has been altered. This trial, so damaging to the reputation of Jews for millennia, was most likely wholly invented by the writer of the Gospel of Mark, and then copied by Matthew and Luke to implicate the Jews in the murder of Jesus, when really it was a Roman affair from beginning to end. Based on the traces left in the text, the trials were almost certainly fabrications designed to indict the Jews and exonerate the Romans.

CHAPTER 15

JESUS' CRIMES

Now that we know what the Gospel editors were trying to hide, what were they actually trying to prove? They were trying to establish that Jesus was not a political rebel but a religious one; that his rebellion was against the Jews rather than the Romans.

Historically, Christianity has maintained that Jesus was put to death by the rabbis for religious crimes: healing on the Sabbath, claiming to be the messiah, blaspheming against God, predicting the destruction of the Temple, and attempting to abolish Jewish law. All these charges are intended to show him as a religious rebel. Yet, upon closer examination, all show something very different.

BREAKING THE SABBATH

The Gospels allege a major motive for having Jesus killed was the Jews' anger at his engaging in healing on the Sabbath.[154] And yet Jesus defends himself vigorously against any charge that he violated the Sabbath with arguments derived from Pharisaic writings. As we noted earlier, these arguments appear in the Talmud and are supported by Jewish law. Any contemporary Orthodox rabbi would rule as Jesus did: when life is threatened, the Sabbath must be violated.

Orthodox Jewish doctors today routinely answer their cell phones *even in synagogue* on the Sabbath. They drive to the hospital on the Sabbath in order to heal their patients. As Hyam Maccoby writes in *The Mythmaker*:

When we consult the Pharisee law books to find out what the Pharisees actually taught about healing on the Sabbath, we find that they did not forbid it, and they even used the very same arguments that Jesus used to show that it was permitted. Moreover Jesus' celebrated saying, "The Sabbath was made for man, not man for the Sabbath," which has been hailed so many times as an epoch-making new insight proclaimed by Jesus, is found almost word for word in a Pharisee source [Talmud tractate Yoma 85b], where it is used to support the Pharisee doctrine that the saving of life has precedence over the law of the Sabbath.[155]

In other words, if we look to Jewish law, breaking the Sabbath is not only allowed but necessary when lives are at stake. When Jesus healed on the Sabbath, he was following the standard, Orthodox, Pharisaic practice.

Why would the Pharisees want Jesus condemned to death for something they themselves preached and practiced? As we have already discussed, when Jesus' disciples picked corn on the Sabbath, for which Jesus received a strong rebuke from the Pharisees, Jesus responded by comparing his disciples' situation to that of David when David was in life-and-death flight from King Saul. In effect he was saying: My students are starving to death, so I have allowed them to pick corn on the Sabbath.

This indirectly supports the theory that Jesus was not a religious rebel but a political one, hotly pursued by the Romans. He gave a rabbinical ruling that explained that his students had sufficient grounds for breaking the Sabbath. Had his students not been in a life-threatening situation – being pursued by the political powers of the country – Jesus' analogy to David's situation would have made little sense. Like David, Jesus knew his situation was perilous. The Romans and their Jewish collaborators sought to kill him because of his views against the imperial throne. Thus, breaking the Sabbath was in no way a reason for Jesus to be condemned to death. Indeed, Jesus' arguments about healing on the Sabbath lead to an opposite conclusion: he was a devoted Pharisee rabbi learned in Pharisaic sources.

ASPIRING TO BE THE MESSIAH

The second pillar of supposed rabbinic anger toward Jesus was founded on Jesus' claim to be the long-promised messiah. No question, Jesus hoped he was sent to save his people from oppression. However, contrary to what even most contemporary Christians believe about Judaism, proclaiming oneself the messiah does not constitute a sin. Indeed, many have made this precise claim throughout Jewish history without any negative repercussions.

Bar Kochba, who led a Jewish rebellion against Rome some one hundred years after Jesus' death, declared himself the messiah and was supported by the greatest rabbis of his day, including Rabbi Akiva, the leading Second Temple rabbinic authority. In the words of the Jerusalem Talmud, "Akiva expounded the following verse homiletically: 'A star will come out of Jacob,'[156] and so nicknamed the rebel as *Kochba*, 'the Star,' rather than *Kozeiva*, his actual name. When Akiva would see Bar Kochba, he would say: '*Dein hu Malka Meshicha!*' (This is the King Messiah!)."[157]

Yet the Bar Kochba rebellion failed. Akiva's opponent Rabbi Joshua ben Korchah reproved him, "Akiva, grass will grow through your cheekbones, and the messiah will still not have come."[158] He was unfortunately correct. For Akiva's resistance against Rome and support of Bar Kochba, Akiva was flayed alive.

I have written elsewhere, in both columns and books, encouraging every person to *aspire* to be the messiah. Okay, if not the actual, big-cheese messiah then little messiahs, who redeem their small corner of the world. We should all strive to bring about a state of redemption. We should all work for peace, harmony, and healing. Curing disease, ending human suffering, bringing peace to our surroundings – all part of the messiah's mission – are the sorts of activities we should all engage in vigorously, often, and everywhere. Even if we fail and don't actually become *the* messiah, we will still have made a difference for the betterment of us all.

Of the Jewish historical figures who claimed to be the messiah – each treated either as an eccentric or a serious candidate, depending on his righteousness, actions, and accomplishments – not one faced execution. It's no big deal to declare yourself the messiah. You just have to back it up with the fulfillment of the messianic prophecies, something Jesus tried to do by redeeming the Jews from political servitude to an oppressive Roman master.

Christians seem to think that Jews perceive self-proclamation as the messiah as blasphemy, perhaps because Christians understand the messiah to be a deity. Yet this is in stark contrast to the Jewish definition of the term and fails to reflect the understanding of Jesus and his contemporaries.

The Jews believe "messiah" to be the title given to a very wise Jewish king who reestablishes Jewish sovereignty in Israel and brings truth and justice to the world, ending war and hunger. Judaism has a standard procedure for responding to an individual who announces he is the messiah: wait and see what happens. The Jewish community reviews whether or not the person in question fulfills the messianic prophecies – ends war and gathers in the dispersed remnants of the Jewish people. If the person succeeds in fulfilling the prophecies, his messiahship becomes confirmed. If he fails, we take it as a sign that the would-be claimant may be righteous, perhaps even a prophet, but certainly not the messiah.

It is worth quoting here from Maimonides' Laws of Kings,[159] where he details the qualifications and necessary accomplishments of the messiah, as well as how we treat those who attempt the fulfill-ment of the messianic prophecies but fail:

> 1. The messianic king will arise in the future and restore the Davidic kingdom to its former state and original sovereign-ty. He will build the Sanctuary and gather the dispersed of Is-rael. All the laws will be re-instituted in his days as they had been aforetimes; sacrifices will be offered, and the Sabbatical years and Jubilee years will be observed fully as ordained by the Torah.
>
> Anyone who does not believe in [Mashiach], or whoever does not look forward to his coming, denies not only [the teachings of] the other prophets but [also those] of the Torah and of Moses our Teacher. For the Torah attested to him, as it is said:
>
> "God, your God, will return your captivity and have mercy on you. He will return and gather you [from all the nations whither God, your God, has scattered you]. If your banished shall be at the utmost end of the heavens [God, your God, will gather you from there]…and God, your God, will bring you [to the land that your fathers possessed, and you will possess it]…."
>
> These words, explicitly stated in the Torah, include all the [Messianic] statements made by all the prophets.
>
> There is reference [to this principle] also in the section of *Bilam*. There he prophesied about the two *meshichim* (anointed ones): the first anointed one who is [King] David who saved Israel from the hand of their oppressors; and the final anointed one [i.e., Mashiach] who will arise from [the former's] descendants and save Israel in the end. Thus it says there:
>
> "I see him, but not now" – this refers to David;

"I behold him, but not nigh" – this refers to the messianic king.

"A star steps out from Jacob" – this refers to David;

"and a scepter will arise from Israel" – this refers to the messianic king.

"He will smite the great ones of Moab" – this refers to David, as it says, "He smote Moab and measured them with a rope";

"and break all the children of Seth" – this refers to the messianic king, of whom it is said, "His rule will be from sea to sea."

"Edom will be a possession" – this refers to David, as it is said, "Edom became servants to David;

"[and Seir] shall be a possession" – this refers to the messianic king, as it is said, "Saviors shall ascend Mount Zion [to judge the mount of Esau]."

...

3. Do not think that the messianic king will have to perform signs and wonders and bring about novel things in the world, or resurrect the dead, and other such things. It is not so. This is seen from the fact that Rabbi Akiva was a great sage, of the sages of the Mishnah, and he was an armor-bearer of King Bar Koziba [Bar Kochba] and said of him that he is the Messianic King: [R. Akiva] and all the wise men of his generation considered him to be the messianic king until [Bar Koziba] was killed because of sins, and when he was killed they realized that he was not; but the sages had not asked him for any sign or wonder.

The essence of all this is that this Torah [of ours], its statutes and its laws, are forever and all eternity, and nothing is to be added to them or diminished from them.

(Whoever adds or diminishes anything, or interprets the Torah to change the plain sense of the commandments, is surely an impostor, wicked, and a heretic.)

4. If a king arises from the House of David who meditates on the Torah and occupies himself with the commandments like his ancestor David, in accordance with the written and oral Torah, and he will prevail upon all of Israel to walk in [the ways of the Torah] and strengthen its breaches, and he will fight the battles of God it may be assumed that he is Mashiach.

If he did [these things] *successfully* (and defeated all the nations around him), built the Sanctuary on its site and gathered the dispersed of Israel he is definitely Mashiach! He will [then] correct the entire world to serve God in unity, as it is said, "For then I will turn to the peoples a pure tongue that all shall call upon the Name of God and serve Him with one consent."

(If he did not succeed to that extent or was killed, it is clear that he is not the [Mashiach] promised by the Torah… for all the prophets said that Mashiach is the redeemer of Israel and their savior, and he gathers their dispersed and reinforces their commandments….)

Chapter 12:5. In that era there will be neither famine nor war, neither envy nor strife, because good will emanate in abundance and all delightful things will be accessible as dust. The one preoccupation of the entire world will be solely to know God. The Israelites, therefore, will be great sages and know the hidden matters, and they will attain knowledge of their Creator to the extent of human capacity, as it is said: "The earth shall be full with the knowledge of God as the waters cover the sea!"[160]

As you can see, a messianic applicant, someone who leads the people but fails to win the ultimate victory, must be seen as a failed messiah. Bar Kochba and many others exemplify such failed messiahs. Yet Judaism also typically regards these people as real heroes. We do not vilify them or blame them for failure. For example, we admire Bar Kochba, who bravely fought for Jewish political and religious independence, and who actually achieved it for two years before his reconstituted Jewish state was crushed. But neither a messianic applicant nor a failed messiah would ever be put to death for the claim of being the messiah.

Indeed, several other messianic claimants appeared during the time period of Jesus. Such times and situations bred turbulence and anger. Jews longed for redemption from the oppressive Roman regime. Yet the Jews accused not one of these claimants of blasphemy. In fact, many of them gathered a large Jewish following.

For Jews, the name *messiah* simply means "the anointed" (*christos* means the same thing) and has no connotations whatsoever regarding divinity. (I have written an entire book on Jewish messianism, *The Wolf Shall Lie with the Lamb*,[161] where many of these concepts are explained.) As all Jews would have known during the Second Temple era, the long-promised messianic king had to be a mortal ruler from the House of David, anointed with oil, who restored the Jewish monarchy and political sovereignty. David exemplified the messianic king because he established an independent Jewish kingdom. The messianic claim has absolutely nothing heretical about it.

By claiming to be King Messiah, Jesus made a political rather than a religious statement. He declared his opposition to Rome and rallied the people to his banner to fight for freedom, just as Bar Kochba would do a hundred years later.

By claiming the messianic crown, Jesus did nothing heretical. He would not have been hated or opposed by the rabbis for doing so. At most, he would have been challenged to prove his credentials.

Failing that, he would have been mourned as yet another fallen messianic claimant who had valiantly attempted to redeem his people.

Blaspheming against God

So what about the charge of blasphemy? Didn't the rabbis want Jesus dead because he equated himself with God? The Book of Matthew shows that at the trial of Jesus, the high priest asks Jesus if he is indeed guilty of claiming to be God. Jesus responds, "You will see me at the right hand of the Power." Mel Gibson, in *The Passion of the Christ*, gives this scene great dramatization, as if this were *the* charge for which Jesus was put to death.

But even if this trial did take place – based on the evidence and historical record, it probably did not – Jesus' statement contains absolutely nothing blasphemous. Indeed, Jews would view a statement like this as being quite virtuous insofar as it expresses what millions of Jews have aspired to throughout their lives, namely, to be at the right hand of God. The Talmud is replete with similar statements by great rabbis who wished that when they died they would be beside God's throne. So where is the blasphemy? In his exchange with the high priest, Jesus does not once say he is God, but rather that he is close to God. Indeed, in the book of Deuteronomy, Moses expressly tells the entire Jewish nation, "You are the children of the Lord your God."[162]

But even had Jesus claimed to be God (which is different from claiming to be divine and thus another god), he would not have been charged with blasphemy. Unlike Christianity, Judaism does not associate blasphemy with a person claiming to be God. If a person made such a claim in a Jewish court, he or she would be told to go home and get a good night's rest. Alternately, such a person might be sent to an asylum. But a punishment of death would never have been issued because absolutely no one would take the claim seriously.

In Judaism, blasphemy involves *cursing* God, not claiming to be God. If you curse God, and you do it in front of a minimum of two witnesses, that is a circumstance under which you can incur the penalty of death. This seemingly small distinction reminds us of what gives Judaism its distinctive character: diligent pursuit of detail out of a love of serving God and a desire to see justice and mercy prevail on earth. Claiming to be God involves no penalty whatsoever, as it would be seen as crazy rather than blasphemous.

So here we are again, wondering what possible religious offense Jesus could have committed in order to warrant a death penalty from the Pharisees or the Sanhedrin. Neither the messianic claim nor the charge of blasphemy would have been impetus for reactions even close to what the New Testament alleges.

DESTROYING THE TEMPLE

The New Testament says Jesus angered the high priest by threatening, or at least predicting, the destruction of the Temple. Jesus said he would have it destroyed and then rebuilt. While surely this would have antagonized the high priest and his entourage, who were the puppets of Rome and used the Temple as their power base, this prediction is the exact same one made by a host of Jewish prophets. Each said God would destroy the Temple because the Jews had become sinful and the priesthood corrupt.

Ezekiel's prophecy describes an angry God willing to kill His people and destroy Jerusalem for their idolatry. He quotes God as saying, "The sin of the people of Israel and Judah is exceedingly great; the land is full of bloodshed and the city is full of injustice. They say, 'The Lord has forsaken the land; the Lord does not see.' So I will not look on them with pity or spare them, but I will bring down on their own heads what they have done."[163] Jeremiah repeatedly predicted the destruction of the First Temple, quoting God's warning to the

Jews, "What I did to Shiloh I will now do to the house that bears My Name, the temple you trust in, the place I gave to you and your ancestors. I will thrust you from My presence, just as I did all your fellow Israelites, the people of Ephraim."[164] Even so, Jeremiah is revered to this day as one of the greatest Jewish prophets.

Indeed, the Pharisees, like Jesus himself, were becoming increasingly disillusioned with the Jerusalem Temple because it had been taken over by crooked, Roman-selected priests. The very first thing the Pharisees did during the revolt of 66 CE, when they had a brief respite from Roman rule, was to dismiss the fraudulent, Roman-appointed high priest and replace him with one uncontaminated by collaboration with Rome. So certain were the rabbis that the Temple could not survive Jewish sinfulness that Rabbi Yochanan ben Zakai, the leading sage at the time of the destruction of the Second Temple, did not even request that the Temple to be spared.

Instead, as the Talmud tells the story, Rabbi Yochanan went to the camp of the Roman commander, Vespasian. "When he reached the Romans he said, 'Peace to you, O king, peace to you, O king.' He [Vespasian] said: 'Your life is forfeit on two counts, one because I am not a king and you call me king, and again, if I am a king, why did you not come to me before now?' He replied: 'As for your saying that you are not a king, in truth you are a king, since if you were not a king Jerusalem would not be delivered into your hand, as it is written.'" Vespasian disbelieved him, but sure enough, a messenger soon arrived to inform him that the emperor had died and he was to take his place as head of state. In great wonder at Rabbi Yochanan's prophetic cleverness, Vespasian offered him a wish. "He said, 'I am now going, and will send someone to take my place. You can, however, make a request of me and I will grant it.' He [Rabbi Yochanan] said to him: 'Give me Yavneh and its wise men.'"[165]

Rabbi Yochanan thought the Temple was beyond saving. He therefore requested instead that the city of Yavneh be spared as a Jewish academy of Torah study – and so it was.

At the time of his death, Jesus had emerged as yet another in a long and great chain of prophets and sages who predicted the Temple's destruction and its rebuilding. Not only was predicting the destruction of the Temple uncontroversial, it was positively virtuous, since it emphasized God's refusal to reside among a people that had become impure. Going back to the time of Moses, prophets had predicted that if the Jewish people were sinful God would remove His presence from among them.

As to the theme of the rebuilding of the Temple, the prophet Ezekiel, who lived about three hundred years before Jesus, predicted that the Second Temple, which was about to be built, would not last, and that God would send a Third Temple down from the heavens. In his prophecy, Ezekiel draws us into the vision, saying:

> In visions of God he took me to the land of Israel and set me on a very high mountain, on whose south side were some buildings that looked like a city. He took me there, and I saw a man whose appearance was like bronze; he was standing in the gateway with a linen cord and a measuring rod in his hand. The man said to me, "Son of man, look carefully and listen closely and pay attention to everything I am going to show you, for that is why you have been brought here. Tell the people of Israel everything you see."[166]

Ezekiel then spends many chapters giving minute details of how the Third Temple will look.

Jesus continued in this long tradition of complaint against the inadequacy of the Second Temple. He envisioned its eventual replacement by the Third Temple that would descend from the heavens, where it had been built. Therefore, the rabbis would never have persecuted Jesus for predicting the destruction of the Temple. They knew the theme and supported the insistence that the nation of Israel become more uniformly righteous and turn away from sinfulness. The rabbis shared and spoke messages similar to what Jesus taught.

CHANGING THE LAW

The only remaining religious charge for which Jesus could possibly have been prosecuted is seeking to change the Law of Moses. The law, of course, is of divine origin. Exodus recounts the story of God issuing the first laws directly to the nation of Israel. The Law of Moses includes the teachings concerning the ways in which we may observe the laws and be holy. The Gospels try to depict tension between Jesus and the rabbis over his reinterpretation of classical Jewish teachings. The texts as they are read today portray Jesus as having been in opposition to the Law of Moses on such things as the concept of "an eye for an eye," divorce, and the dietary laws.

But this portrayal is the most unfounded of all.

If the Gospels show us anything about Jesus, it is that he was utterly dedicated to adhering to the Law of Moses, both in teaching and in practice. As I have quoted previously from Matthew, Jesus famously says those who don't keep every last letter of the Torah will be the least in the kingdom of heaven. He adds that anyone who argues for abrogating the law would be held in deep contempt by heaven.

As for the famous teaching in the Sermon on the Mount that "an eye for an eye" should not be taken literally, this was (and still is) classic Pharisaic, rabbinic teaching. Indeed, this teaching demonstrates again that Jesus was a devout Pharisee. To the Jews both in Jesus' time and well before his time, these words signified that monetary compensation should be owed for an eye rather than a vengeful extraction of the eye itself, as even a child in a Jewish school can tell you. The ancient rabbis regarded the expression "an eye for an eye" as a symbolic demonstration of the seriousness of any injury perpetrated against one's fellow man. The monetary restitution had to be in accordance with the injury. The expression never meant the perpetrator should be blinded. Teachings such as these had been passed down from God to Moses to Joshua and beyond, an unbroken chain of transmission and receiving. These teachings helped the Jewish nation understand how to live the Torah and serve God lovingly.

Likewise, Jesus never abolished the dietary laws, contrary to some claims made about him. Jesus makes it absolutely clear that "I have kept my Father's commands."[167] What he says about these laws, called *kashrut*, is this: "Listen and understand: What goes into someone's mouth does not defile them, but what comes out of their mouth, that is what defiles them."[168] This teaching focuses on the ethical defilement of that which emanates from someone's mouth. Clearly, a person who does not keep kosher may not be religious, but that does not equate to being unethical. Using one's tongue to assassinate the character of an innocent victim, on the other hand, is immoral. What one eats is a matter of spiritual commitments, and Jesus was a completely kosher Jew. But what comes out of one's mouth – improper talk and conversation – has the capacity to corrode one's character.

Again, this is classic Jewish teaching. The prohibitions on slander, gossip, blasphemy, and using foul and unclean language date back to the Bible itself. The Hebrew Bible says clearly, "Do not go about spreading slander among your people."[169] Similarly, Proverbs says, "The words of the reckless pierce like swords, but the tongue of the wise brings healing."[170] Elsewhere the Psalmist says, "May these words of my mouth and this meditation of my heart be pleasing in your sight, Lord, my Rock and my Redeemer."[171] We find the same sentiment no fewer than three times in Proverbs: "The hearts of the wise make their mouths prudent, and their lips promote instruction."[172] "One who loves a pure heart and who speaks with grace will have the king for a friend."[173] And, "My son, if your heart is wise, then my heart will be glad indeed; my inmost being will rejoice when your lips speak what is right."[174]

So all Jesus says is that *in addition* to being careful not to abrogate the Jewish ritualistic laws, which he himself was vigilant to observe, one must also be careful with the ethical laws. Violating *kashrut* constitutes a transgression, and impure and unjust speech belittles the speaker.

Many of Jesus' sayings focus on individuals minding their tongues, speaking with charity, kindness, and mercy – all fundamental Jewish principles. The same is true of divorce. Jesus was not just an observant Jew. He was extremely pious in his observance. Like many Hasidic Jews today, Jesus went beyond the letter of the law, which is what "Hasid" means in Hebrew. So, whereas the Torah allows divorce, Jesus does not countenance it. Whereas the Torah calls adultery a transgression of the body, Jesus says one is just as culpable if it is an act of the mind. He doesn't want his people even *thinking* of that kind of sinfulness. The great Jewish sage Maimonides said the same thing: that even lusting after a forbidden sexual relationship constitutes a transgression. God demands purity of body *and* mind. You would find the same strictures among Hasidic Jews today who only in the rarest circumstances permit divorce, and who insist on cleanliness of thought as well as of deed.

Jesus grew up and began his ministry in the Galilee, where the most staunchly religious Jews lived. The Galilee was also the region that constantly fomented rebellion against Rome. He was a political rebel and religious pietist who observed Jewish law to the highest degree. Virtually everything Jesus taught was based on classical biblical, Pharisaic, and Talmudic teaching. Not only did he *not* break from the Torah, he sought to reestablish Torah observance over the course of his campaign for spiritual renewal and political liberation.

Nowhere is this better illustrated than in the Sermon on the Mount. Here we see that everything Jesus taught had a biblical and rabbinic origin. Jesus was a master *darshan* (orator), an exegete who could take biblical teachings and put them in powerfully personal words. That's what made him such an effective communicator and teacher. And Jesus' most famous teachings and celebrated proverbs have their origin in earlier biblical texts.

Here I offer some of Jesus' most famous teachings and their sources in earlier Scripture:

> **Jesus**: Blessed are the meek, for they will inherit the earth. (Matthew 5:5)

> **Bible**: The meek will inherit the earth, and enjoy peace and prosperity. (Psalms 37:11)

> **Jesus**: Blessed are the pure in heart, for they will see God. (Matthew 5:8)

> **Bible**: Who may ascend the mountain of the Lord? Who may stand in his holy place? The one who has clean hands and a pure heart. (Psalms 24:3–4)

> **Jesus**: If anyone slaps you on the right cheek, turn to them the other cheek also. (Matthew 5:39)

> **Bible**: Let him offer his cheek to one who would strike him… (Lamentations 3:30)

> **Jesus**: But seek first His kingdom and His righteousness, and all these things will be given to you as well. (Matthew 6:33)

> **Bible**: Take delight in the Lord, and he will give you the desires of your heart. (Psalms 37:4)

Jesus: Ask and it will be given to you; seek and you will find; knock and the door will be opened to you. (Matthew 7:7)

Bible: You will seek me and find me when you seek me with all your heart. (Jeremiah 29:13)

Jesus: Then I will tell them plainly, 'I never knew you. Away from me, you evildoers!' (Matthew 7:23)

Bible: Away from me, all you who do evil... (Psalms 6:8)

Jesus: Do not give dogs what is sacred; do not throw your pearls to pigs. If you do, they may trample them under their feet, and turn and tear you to pieces. (Matthew 7:6)

Bible: Do not speak to fools, for they will scorn your prudent words. (Proverbs 23:9)

If Jesus was such a devout Pharisee and rabbi, then, why would the Jews want him dead? The truth is: they didn't. *The rabbis had no problem whatsoever with Jesus.* Indeed, they rightly thought of him as one of their own, one who espoused core teachings with which they all fundamentally agreed. This is the reason why Luke 31 clearly says that the rabbis saved Jesus' life when Herod sought to kill him, as detailed above. The principal dissenting voice, who argued that Jesus came to uproot the teachings of Judaism and therefore incurred the ire of the rabbis, who wanted him dead, turns out to be the most consequential of all, Paul of Tarsus. But who was this enigmatic Paul, and was he correct in his assertions?

CHAPTER 16

PAUL THE PHARISEE?

The most influential figure in the changing of the Jesus narrative was Paul of Tarsus. He is the filter through whom Christianity reached the world. More than anyone else, he is responsible for recasting Jesus' teachings in a light palatable to gentiles, thoroughly redefining and revising Jesus' thought. Had Paul's mission to the gentiles failed, Jesus would have been another valiant Jewish rebel leader the Romans had put to death. However, Paul transformed Jesus' mission and made him into a global historical figure. To understand the changes he made to Jesus' personality, we must also understand Paul.

We would do well to begin with his own words. Paul tells us he was a Pharisee sent by the Jewish high priest to persecute Christians in Damascus. He claims to have converted to a belief in Jesus after an epiphany while on the road to the Assyrian city. Here he introduces himself:

> I am a Jew, born in Tarsus of Cilicia, but brought up in this city. I studied under Gamaliel and was thoroughly trained in the law of our ancestors. I was just as zealous for God as any of you are today. I persecuted the followers of this Way to their death, arresting both men and women and throwing them into prison, as the high priest and all the Council can themselves testify. I even obtained letters from them to their associates in Damascus, and went there to bring these

people as prisoners to Jerusalem to be punished. About noon
as I came near Damascus, suddenly a bright light from heaven flashed around me.[175]

At face value, Paul's account is troublesome. First, it's unlikely Paul was a Pharisee or that he studied with Gamliel, the most advanced Pharisaic teacher of the time. By claiming status as a student of Gamliel, Paul is bestowing an impressive honor upon himself, for only the most highly regarded scholars in all of Israel were chosen to sit at the feet of this renowned rabbinic leader who is famous till today.

The Pharisees were great scholars, as any reading of their most important works – the Mishnah and Talmud – will demonstrate. Yet, as Hyam Maccoby points out, Paul is not only not a great scholar, he seems incapable of even reading Hebrew. When Paul quotes from the Hebrew Bible in his epistles, he uses the Greek Septuagint translation rather than the Hebrew. There are many situations in which the Hebrew Bible and the Septuagint translation differ considerably. Whenever they do, Paul follows the faulty Greek translation rather than the original Hebrew.[176] No disciple of Gamliel would have thought to read the Bible in translation; there would have been no need.

Paul's letters to the Corinthians offer excellent examples of the resulting inaccuracies. Paul quotes Hosea 13:14, saying, "Where, O death, is your victory? Where, O death, is your sting?"[177] This is the version found in the Greek Septuagint. But the Hebrew original reads: "Where, O death, are your plagues? Where, O grave, is your destruction?" The Septuagint's mistranslation changes the meaning completely. Paul's words are rife with such mistranslations, some of them affecting the most important tenets of Christian belief.

Paul's mistakes make parts of the Christian doctrine he devised problematic. For example, one of Paul's most monumental claims is that Jewish law is no longer applicable after Jesus. He argues in

Galatians that the Law of Moses has been rendered obsolete by Jesus' death on the cross. Jesus has fulfilled the law and atoned for the sins of mankind. This is an astonishing claim given that Jesus himself said, as we quoted earlier, that anyone who doesn't keep every last letter of the law will be last in the kingdom of heaven.

To prove his case, Paul quotes from a law in Deuteronomy. According to Paul's citation, Moses tells the Jewish people that if someone is given capital punishment, the body should be hung on a tree as a deterrent to the rest of the people, but it should not remain there overnight: "You must not leave his body on the tree overnight. Be sure to bury him that same day, because *anyone who is hung on a tree is a curse to God.* You must not desecrate the land the Lord your God is giving you as an inheritance."[178]

The verse's meaning is simple enough. The Bible declares that all people, even criminals, are created in the image of God. To leave a carcass on a tree to rot undermines the dignity of the human person. Even a criminal must be buried properly, as a human body created in God's image is holy. However, Paul misrepresents the verse utterly. He says, "Christ redeemed us from the curse of the law by becoming a curse for us, for it is written: 'Cursed is everyone who is hung on a pole.'"[179] Paul misquotes the Bible and gives it a fraudulent meaning. He explains that the pole refers to the Torah, the Law of Moses. If you hang on this pole – that is, if you are dependent on the law for salvation rather than the blood of Christ – you are cursed.

Paul's understanding is an allegorical stretch that completely robs the verse of its original meaning. This is all due to a simple mistranslation. The verse makes it plain that it is a curse "to God," not man, to hang the body on a tree. God created humans in His image, and if you desecrate a human body it is therefore an affront to God. Moreover, the verse in Deuteronomy does not even refer to the Torah or Moses' law. It refers explicitly to capital punishment. It is troubling that Paul bases one of Christianity's core doctrines on a misrepresentation. Nonetheless, this leads Paul to his conclusion later in the same chapter of Galatians, "Now that faith has come, we are no longer under a guardian."[180] That is to say, the law no longer applies. One shudders at the idea that Christians for millennia have followed the teachings of Paul against the express teachings of Jesus based on Paul's errant rendering of a very straightforward biblical verse.

Imagine the implications of just one important commandment, the Sabbath, which Christians no longer observe according to the biblical command or even on the biblical day, all because Paul says that the law has been abrogated. God rested on Saturday, not Sunday. Indeed, if the purpose of the Sabbath is the consecration of rest rather than work, then what sense can it make to observe the Sabbath on Sunday when God did the most work, creating heaven and earth itself?

Although it is clear from Paul's statements that he could never have been a Pharisee, further proof is found in the text of the New Testament. A passage of Paul's writing from Romans clearly indicates he was not a Pharisaic scholar.

> Do you not know, brothers and sisters – for I am speaking to those who know the law – that the law has authority over someone only as long as that person lives? For example, by law a married woman is bound to her husband as long as he is alive, but if her husband dies, she is released from the law that binds her to him. So then, if she has sexual relations with another man while her husband is still alive, she is called an adulteress. But if her husband dies, she is released from that law and is not an adulteress if she marries another man. So, my brothers and sisters, you also died to the law through the body of Christ, that you might belong to another, to him who was raised from the dead, in order that we

might bear fruit for God. For when we were in the realm of
the flesh, the sinful passions aroused by the law were at work
in us, so that we bore fruit for death. But now, by dying to
what once bound us, we have been released from the law so
that we serve in the new way of the Spirit, and not in the old
way of the written code.[181]

Paul, as always, writes beautifully. His words are pure poetry. But
they are also utterly nonsensical and contain the most twisted logic.
When read openly and thoughtfully, this passage shows Paul's logic
is beset by his preconceptions, making it utterly contrived – if not altogether incoherent. He begins by comparing the Jewish people to a
widow, and the Torah, the law, to her husband. If the husband dies,
then the woman is allowed to remarry, because the law, her husband,
is dead. But then he says it is not the law that died, but the *people*
who have passed away: "So, my brothers and sisters, *you* also died to
the law…" And then, that *the dead woman*, representing the people,
can marry another man, "that you might belong to another…"

Paul's argument is so confused that he suggests a dead woman
should get remarried. It is nonsensical, and not at all characteristic of a Pharisaic sage whose distinguishing characteristic was razor-
sharp legal logic. But we understand what Paul is trying to do. He is
attempting a conceptual jujitsu – one of the most striking examples
of "outside the box" thinking we are likely to find in the New Testament. Paul is attempting to reinterpret and reinscribe the law to fit
his existing religious ideology. But it's not Jewish thinking, not the
method of a Pharisaic sage, and certainly not the approach a Pharisee such as Jesus would have adopted.

It goes without saying that Paul was not a stupid man. On the
contrary, his letters are brilliant works of art and rhetoric. He ranks
with the most eloquent and daring men of history. I find many of his
letters beautiful to read. But he is as far from a Pharisaic scholar as

one could be. His claims to Pharisaic scholarship and being a disciple of Gamliel are uncorroborated and almost certainly untrue.

AN ENFORCER IN DAMASCUS

Paul claims he was sent by the high priest to persecute the Christians of Damascus. If true, this makes it highly unlikely that he was either a Pharisee or a student of Gamliel. The Pharisees were Jewish nationalists. The high priest and his henchman were allied with Rome; they were Roman muscle, pure and simple. The two groups were mortal enemies and detested one another. When Paul says he worked for the high priest in persecuting the Christians, it means he was a Roman enforcer by proxy. This aligns with his assertion that he was a citizen of Rome.[182] It also explains why Paul could pursue Christians in Damascus.

As Maccoby points out, if Paul were really a messenger sent by Gamliel to persecute the Christians, he would have no jurisdiction in Damascus, where King Arêtes was ruler. However, if Paul worked for the high priest as an agent of Rome, his presence in Damascus makes much better sense. King Arêtes was also a Roman proxy and Damascus a Roman province. A Roman ally would permit the high priest's guards into his territory to pursue a Jewish rebel group opposed to Roman dominance.

Paul outright contradicts himself on this subject. He says first that he was a student of Gamliel, but then tells us he was sent to Damascus by the high priest.

> I too was convinced that I ought to do all that was possible to oppose the name of Jesus of Nazareth. And that is just what I did in Jerusalem. On the authority of the chief priests I put many of the Lord's people in prison, and when they were put to death, I cast my vote against them. Many a time

I went from one synagogue to another to have them punished, and I tried to force them to blaspheme. I was so obsessed with persecuting them that I even hunted them down in foreign cities. On one of these journeys I was going to Damascus with the authority and commission of the chief priests.[183]

This contradiction is significant. Paul is the main exponent of the idea that Jesus was a religious rather than political rebel. Paul overturns nearly all of Jesus' teachings by saying that Jesus came to change Judaism and abolish the law, whereas Jesus himself says in Matthew 5:18 that every last letter of the Torah must be strictly observed. Paul justifies his abrogation of the law by saying Jesus' death fulfilled the law, but his credentials as an interpreter of Scripture are minimal. Not only that, but his expertise as an interpreter of the life and teachings of Jesus, if we may be honest, is nonexistent.

PAUL THE CONVERT

It is even possible, as Hyam Maccoby maintains, that Paul was not born Jewish but converted. This would explain his bizarre claim that he belongs to a particular tribe of Israel. His excessive efforts to validate his own Jewishness certainly raise a red flag.

In Romans, Paul describes his Jewish identity to an extraordinary degree of specificity. "I am an Israelite myself, a descendant of Abraham, from the tribe of Benjamin."[184] This statement verges on the absurd given that by Paul's time, the tribe of Benjamin was no longer distinguishable from the rest of the Jews. The only identifiable groups within Judaism were the tribe of Judah (which is where the word Jew comes from) and the tribe of Levi, consisting of priests and levites. As Hyam Maccoby writes, "While it is true that part of the tribe of Benjamin survived in Palestine after the deportation of the

Ten Tribes by Shalmaneser of Assyria, the Benjaminites later intermarried with the tribe of Judah to such an extent that they lost their separate identity and all became Judahites, or Jews."[185]

The belief that Paul was a convert to Judaism dates back to the time immediately following Jesus' death. The Ebionites, the remnants of the Jerusalem Church under the leadership of James (whom the New Testament and Josephus say was Jesus' own brother), insisted that Paul was a non-Jew who had converted to Judaism. Maccoby reports that "according to the Ebionites, Saul was not a Pharisee and not even a Jew by birth. His parents in Tarsus were gentiles, and he himself had become a convert and had thereupon journeyed to the Holy Land, where he found employment in the service of the high priest."[186]

Paul always claimed legitimacy regarding Christianity because he had been a tireless persecutor of the early Church who later joined the Christians. This is a point he makes often. In Galatians he expands on that theme once again: "For you have heard of my previous way of life in Judaism, how intensely I persecuted the church of God and tried to destroy it. I was advancing in Judaism beyond many of my own age and was extremely zealous for the traditions of my fathers."[187]

Paul is doing his best to convince his readers he was a Pharisee upholding the law. However, he is trying so hard his efforts draw attention to themselves. If anything, Paul seems to be a fanatic. He had hated the Christians with relish, and even incriminated himself by saying he goaded them into blaspheming. What could have made him hate the Christians so much that he volunteered for long journeys to persecute them? This is one of the great mysteries of Paul's claims. He seems to be a brilliant but unstable character prone to manic extremes.

PAUL'S INTENTIONS

According to all indications in the synoptic Gospels, Jesus was a devoutly religious Jew, who kept all the Jewish rituals and stated repeatedly that he was sent only for "the lost sheep of Israel."[188] Yet Paul transformed Jesus' mission into one that actively excluded the Jews, restricting him almost exclusively to the gentiles. Jesus' early followers didn't approve. They considered Paul's innovations so offensive that he incurred the opprobrium of the Jerusalem Church for being a radical reformer of Jesus' original message.[189]

When viewed in light of Paul's true identity, such a mission makes a lot more sense. He radically shifted Jesus' message away from politics and toward religion. Whereas Jesus preached to reinforce Judaism, Paul preached to abrogate it. Jesus came to rebel against Rome. Paul, the Roman citizen, absolves the Romans from killing Jesus and blames the Jews instead. Jesus loved his people and devoted himself to their welfare. But Paul made Jesus and the Jews into bitter enemies, as is clear from statements like this:

> For you, brothers, became imitators of God's churches in Judea, which are in Christ Jesus. You suffered from your own people the same things those churches suffered from the Jews, who killed the Lord Jesus and the prophets and also drove us out. They displease God and are hostile to everyone in their effort to keep us from speaking to the gentiles so that they may be saved. In this way they always heap up their sins to the limit. The wrath of God has come upon them at last.[190]

Here, Paul's words drip with animosity toward Jews.

Jesus wanted to deliver the Jews from Rome. Paul wanted only to deliver them from Judaism. Furthermore, Jesus was exclusively interested in the Jewish people, while Paul was obsessed with proselytizing gentiles.

In the end, Paul created a myth of Jesus that persists until today. Paul even expresses his approval of such dishonesty, claiming he did it all "for the sake of the Gospel, that I may share in its blessings."[191]

His argument that he was allowed to deceive in order to save souls smacks of the worst kind of the-end-justifies-the-means argument. As he himself says:

> Though I am free and belong to no one, I have made myself a slave to everyone, to win as many as possible. To the Jews I became like a Jew, to win the Jews. To those under the law I became like one under the law (though I myself am not under the law), so as to win those under the law. To those not having the law I became like one not having the law (though I am not free from God's law but am under Christ's law), so as to win those not having the law. To the weak I became weak, to win the weak. I have become all things to all people so that by all possible means I might save some.[192]

With Paul's rationalization that he may deceive in order to achieve his aims of "saving" others – that is, bring them into his Church – we can reasonably say he would have had no compunction about pretending to be a Pharisee to win over Pharisee converts to Jesus, even though he was a Sadducee prior to converting to Christianity. After all, for Paul, we are all sinners. We can't change it or do anything about it. Even if we were to try we would fail. So, Paul reasons, only faith in the idea that Jesus could act as a human sacrifice can absolve sin (an anathema to Jews, which we will explore in further detail in later chapters).

For Paul, it is all about faith. A misrepresentation or two to persuade people to join in the faith is no big deal. Faith always balances the scales for the sinner in the end. As we shall see, Paul's doctrines were entirely foreign to the early followers of Jesus, as they would have been to Jesus himself.

CHAPTER 17

PAUL AND THE ORIGINAL APOSTLES

Paul's claims about who Jesus was and what he preached are made more tenuous by the sheer scope of his deviations from the lessons of Jesus' own followers. The leaders of the Jerusalem Church, Peter and James, insisted that Jesus' message was for Jews and was dedicated to preserving Jewish law and observance. Paul transformed that message completely.

Paul claimed to know better what Jesus intended than the disciples whom Jesus taught directly – even though Paul never even met Jesus. He said that Jesus meant to abolish Jewish law, that faith is more important than works, and that the sole criteria for salvation is faith in Christ. Not only that, Paul added that Jesus was not mortal, and his claim to be the messiah meant that he was the divine son of God. Finally, Paul, a self-declared Roman citizen, shifts the developing faith of Jesus, Christianity, to be pro-Roman and anti-Jewish. Paul attacks Judaism as antiquated and obsolete, and to cap it all off, he accuses the Jews of killing Jesus, also claiming they attacked him personally on many occasions.

This is an unabashed distortion of Jesus' teachings. It was opposed by all the original disciples. Yet, through eloquence and persistence, Paul becomes the spiritual successor of Jesus, and the midwife – some would say, true father – of Christianity. He abrogates the Torah and goes against Jesus' insistence that he came only for Israel. Paul shifts Jesus' mission so it specifically targets the gentiles, emphasizing faith is all that matters: "The blessing given to Abraham might come to the gentiles through Christ Jesus, so that by faith we might receive the promise of the Spirit."[193]

Paul met strong opposition from Jesus' leading disciples, including Jesus' successor and brother, James. Unable to dissuade Paul from preaching to gentiles that the Torah no longer mattered, the apostles were reduced to pleading with him to pretend he still kept the law in Jerusalem. In the Book of Acts, Christ's followers sound almost desperate when they say to Paul, "You see, brother, how many thousands of Jews have believed, and all of them are zealous for the law. They have been informed that you teach all the Jews who live among the gentiles to turn away from Moses, telling them not to circumcise their children or live according to our customs. What shall we do?"[194]

The apostles never wavered in their commitment to Judaism, and are stunned that Paul would do so. They voice to Paul their shock that he would tell Jews not to keep the Law of Moses. In the same passage they say, "So do what we tell you. There are four men with us who have made a vow. Take these men, join in their purification rites, and pay their expenses, so that they can have their heads shaved. Then everybody will know there is no truth in these reports about you, but that you yourself are living in obedience to the law. As for the gentile believers, we have written to them our decision that they should abstain from food sacrificed to idols, from blood, from the meat of strangled animals and from sexual immorality."[195]

The apostles are happy to strike a compromise, so long as it is founded on established law. The tenets they are referring to in this passage come from a Pharisaic code called the Noahide Covenant, a system of biblical laws applicable to non-Jews. According to the Talmud, this consists of the Bible's outline of seven laws that God gave Noah; these bind all his descendants and constitute the minimum level of morality to which everyone should adhere. The laws are prohibitions against idolatry, sexual immorality, theft, murder, cruelty to animals, blasphemy against God, and a positive commandment to establish courts that can enforce justice. The apostles are advocating for this Pharisaic code. The prohibition against blood encompasses murder. The prohibition against eating strangled animals refers to avoiding inhumanely slaughtering food. The prohibition of all things connected with idolatry establishes a ban against worshipping anything but God and includes cursing God.

According to Edward Gibbon in *The Decline and Fall of the Roman Empire*, the first ten bishops of the Jerusalem Church were all circumcised Jews, so it is reasonable that they would enforce the Noahide laws. In this early incarnation, Christianity was a Torah-based religion that embraced all aspects of Judaism. At that time, its only addition was to maintain that the messiah, a man of flesh and blood named Jesus, had already come.

This explains why Paul's conduct so shocked the Jerusalem Church. Even Peter, once he began agreeing with Paul and eating non-kosher food, pretended he still observed the law for fear of being ostracized by the rest of the apostles. As Paul writes:

> When Cephas [Peter] came to Antioch, I opposed him to his face, because he stood condemned. For before certain men came from James, he used to eat with the gentiles. But when they arrived, he began to draw back and separate himself from the gentiles because he was afraid of those who belonged to the circumcision group. The other Jews joined him in his hypocrisy, so that by their hypocrisy even Barnabas was led astray. When I saw that they were not acting in line with the truth of the Gospel, I said to Cephas [Peter] in front of them all, "You are a Jew, yet you live like a gentile and not like a Jew. How is it, then, that you force gentiles to follow Jewish customs?"[196]

Paul, ever the manipulator, bullies Peter into accepting the Pauline liberalism. He tells Peter he is being a hypocrite for eating non-kosher food and preaching kosher to the gentiles.

We saw earlier that Peter, unfortunately, often says one thing and does another, so it may not be surprising that Paul again accuses him of hypocrisy. Still, the author of Acts understands that Peter should not have listened to Paul and eaten food that wasn't kosher against Jesus' direct commands to observe all commandments of the Torah. Therefore, in order to justify Paul's actions, the author of Acts explains how Jesus came to Peter in a vision and told him to eat non-kosher:

> He became hungry and wanted something to eat, and while the meal was being prepared, he fell into a trance. He saw heaven opened and something like a large sheet being let down to earth by its four corners. It contained all kinds of four-footed animals, as well as reptiles of the earth and birds of the air. Then a voice told him, "Get up, Peter. Kill and eat."
>
> "Surely not, Lord!" Peter replied. "I have never eaten anything impure or unclean."
>
> The voice spoke to him a second time, "Do not call anything impure that God has made clean."[197]

While Jesus was alive, he *never* taught that non-kosher food was allowed. When he taught Peter in the flesh, he made sure that Peter was a Torah-observant Jew. Yet after Jesus' death, Peter has a dream in which Jesus conveniently contradicts himself.

Why would he believe the dream over Jesus' direct instructions? This seems, if anything, a case of Freudian wish-fulfillment. Peter wants to eat non-kosher food, but refuses to accept the teachings of Paul over Jesus. Then Jesus comes to Peter in a dream and tells him he can accept Paul's teaching. The dream, to the extent that it happened at all, was not a prophecy, but the fulfillment of Peter's desire to be free of the law.

Peter abandons Jesus' strict commitment to kosher food and the Law of Moses and begins to live like a gentile. Christianity soon follows suit. The new religious sect bases itself on the teachings of Paul, a probable convert to Judaism ignorant of the Torah, who even preaches the Torah's abolishment and does not preach the teachings of Jesus, its original Pharisaic leader.

CHAPTER 18

PLACATING ROME

The truth about Jesus is now becoming all too clear: The early Christians, led by Paul, needed to promote the idea that Jesus was a religious reformer rather than a political rebel. After all, they couldn't upset Rome, which already looked disdainfully on the fledgling Church. The Gospels were therefore edited to purge Jesus of all anti-Roman vitriol, and Jesus' story was edited to reflect a conflict between himself and the Jews. But the transformation didn't stop there.

Even after the crucifixion story went through its first round of editing, the Church continued to change. It actively sought to placate Rome and incorporate Roman customs into Christian practice. This process was expedited after the Roman emperor Constantine converted to Christianity in 312 CE. The Church fathers were prepared to alter the narratives – even the tenets of Christianity – to accommodate the needs of the Roman Empire, as the early Church fathers willingly admit.

In the formative years of Christianity, the Church fathers went to great lengths to rip fetal Christianity away from the Jewish womb in which it had been nourished. After they had done so, they transplanted it into a Roman surrogate. Some of the most important institutions of Christianity that are taken for granted today result from the Church fathers' accommodation of Roman practices.

For example, for the first three hundred years after Jesus, the Christian Sabbath was celebrated on Saturday, not Sunday. It was practiced the way the Jews practiced it, as both observances were derived directly from the Bible, which says God rested on the seventh day, the Sabbath. The fact that Christians celebrate the Sabbath on Sunday, the first day of the week, should strike anyone familiar with the story of creation as puzzling. God created the world in six days and rested on the seventh. On the first day of the week, God created the heaven and earth, the foundation for all existence. This level of activity is hardly restful.

However, the Romans worshipped the sun, and venerated Sun-Day as the holiest day of the week. This was part of the Roman cult of Sol Invictus, the unconquered sun-god whom the Romans worshipped. In 321 CE, Constantine, the emperor that converted Rome to Christianity, ordered the law courts closed on "the venerable day of the sun," decreeing it a day of rest.[198] While Christianity had kept Saturday, the Jewish Sabbath, as sacred for three centuries, no one would defy the Roman Emperor, the greatest patron Christianity had ever had. So, in accordance with Constantine's edict, the Christians went against their own doctrine and adopted Sunday as their sacred day.

I put this question to my friend Dr. Michael Brown in one our public debates. How is it, I asked him, that the Bible makes it clear God rested on Saturday, yet Christians now honor Sunday, a day of explosive creation, as the Sabbath. He said it had to do with Jesus being crucified on a Sunday. But what is the connection? We do not keep the seven-day week because Jesus was murdered but because of the biblical account of creation. And it could not be more explicit. The Sabbath is on Saturday, which is why many Christian groups, like the Seventh Day Adventists, rest on Saturday rather than Sunday.

The day of Christmas was also changed, after centuries of Christian tradition, to accommodate Rome. Until the fourth century, Christians celebrated Jesus' birthday on January 6. However, once again, for the Sol Invictus cult, the most important day of the year was December 25, the festival of Natalis Solis Invicti, the birth – or rebirth – of the sun, when the days would begin to grow perceptibly longer. Christianity changed to appease Roman practice and establish itself as the state religion. The aureole of light crowning the head of the sun-god became the Christian halo. Especially in Eastern Orthodoxy, Jesus and the saints are portrayed with a circular, sun-like halo.

Perhaps the biggest concession of the New Testament authors to Rome was the favorable portrayal of the Romans – that is, when they are mentioned at all. Despite their positively brutal occupation of Judea, the Romans are hardly featured in the Gospels. When they are, they function as benign onlookers, or else, in Jesus' Passion, as hapless tools of the manipulating Pharisees. All things considered, the Romans come across as almost gentlemanly, simply doing their best to keep things running in an orderly manner. They appear to be a civilizing force amidst a tribe of primitive, stubborn Jewish extremists and zealots.

Aside from the obvious injustice of this portrayal, it is, as Hyam Maccoby emphasizes, utterly unhistorical.

Nowadays, we tend to hold a somewhat rosy view of the Romans. In an ancient world populated with barbaric hordes and frenzied cults, what was the Roman Empire if not civilization on the march? We owe the Romans the decorum of the Senate and the beauty of surviving ancient monuments.

However, this does not tell the whole story. Romans cherished war and domination. The axiom by which they prospered was "might makes right." They lived by the sword, ruled by the sword, and made sure that others died by the sword. To understand the real Rome we need not look to the architectural splendor of the Colosseum, but at the barbaric gladiatorial combat that took place within it. The real Rome was to be found not in the carved images of the Arch of Titus, but in the thousands of captured slaves that were dragged in chains through its marble.

Yes, as noted earlier, the Romans possessed a civilized outer veneer, borrowing heavily from the culture of the Greeks, which lent them an air of artistic, poetic, and architectural superiority. But if we just scratch the surface we find an empire whose principal engine consisted of brutal Roman soldiers imposing their will on weaker adversaries.

If Jesus had lived in Nazi Germany, and during the years 1940 to 1945 focused his preaching exclusively on matters of faith while ignoring completely the gas chambers and blitzkrieg that were all around him, would we have considered him a righteous leader? In fact, is this not precisely the argument brought nearly two millennia later against Pope Pius XII, the man said to be Jesus' human representative on earth, regarding his conspicuous silence during the Nazi Holocaust? In his passivity he compromised his own moral integrity.

The Gospels relate that Jesus famously proclaimed, "Render unto Caesar what is Caesar's, and unto God what is God's."[199]

Could Jesus have actually said this? Would the prince of peace have endorsed the right of the Roman emperor to exact cruel and unjust tribute from enslaved peoples throughout the world? Would Jesus *really* have made himself party to the Roman occupation by directly legitimizing and endorsing the Romans' right to invade and occupy Judea and mercilessly slaughter the patriotic Jews who battled for survival? Would Jesus have validated a tyrant's oppression of an innocent people?

Surely a man as great as Jesus would be on the side of the victims rather than their oppressors, and would never have advocated blindly accepting Roman rule. He never would have endorsed the brutal occupiers and become an enemy of his people – unless the story of his life was redacted and redirected by later editors to reflect a love of Rome and contempt for the Jews. This statement of "Render unto Caesar what is Caesar's," asking the Jews to submit to the brutal injustices of Rome, beggars belief. I would go so far as to say that it slanders a good man, and I don't believe Jesus ever said it. Rather, it was put in his mouth, well after his monstrous death at the hands of the Romans, to appease the might of Rome and make the Christian sect appear to be allied with Rome.

Worst of all, early Christian Gospel editors provided the spiritual underpinnings for hatred of Jews, turning Jesus against his people and making him the archetypal anti-Semite. In their hands, Jesus is made to affirm that the Jews will be punished by God for killing their prophets. He derides and denounces them, saying: "You snakes! You brood of vipers! How will you escape being condemned to hell? Therefore I am sending you prophets and wise men and teachers. Some of them you will kill and crucify; others you will flog in your synagogues and pursue from town to town. And so upon you will come all the righteous blood that has been shed on earth, from the blood of righteous Abel to the blood of Zechariah son of Berekiah, whom you murdered between the temple and the altar. I tell you the truth, all this will come upon this generation."[200]

There are many reasons to believe that this verse is a forgery. First of all, common sense dictates this doesn't sound anything like the Jesus we know. These poisonous words, "You snakes! You brood of vipers! How will you escape being condemned to hell?" seem utterly inconsistent with the beautiful teachings on ethics in the Sermon on the Mount about the meek and humble inheriting the earth. Was Jesus really prone to such vulgar outbursts and temper tantrums? Indeed, this later, interpolated Jesus sounds like a man with serious anger issues who can't control his rage.

Jesus' alleged vitriol makes him sound like a religious fanatic who preaches hate. More importantly, there's a glaring error in the statement, which Jesus would have never made. It was not Zechariah son of Berekiah that was put to death near the sanctuary, but Zechariah ben Yehoyada, who lived 324 years later. Jesus, a well-trained scholar, would not have made such an obvious mistake. He would have known the difference between the two prophets. Yet gentile editors with no more than a cursory knowledge of Jewish scripture derived through the Greek Septuagint could have easily made this mistake, as they did elsewhere. This editing results in a depiction of Jesus as both ignorant and anti-Semitic.

There are many other such passages of Jesus spewing hateful invective against his people, all added long after Jesus' death and all designed to distance Jesus from his people, making him more Roman than Jewish. These verses abound especially in the Gospel of John. At one point, Jesus goes so far as to call the Jews Satan's spawn: "You belong to your father, the devil, and you want to carry out your father's desires. He was a murderer from the beginning."[201]

Jesus likewise declares that the Jews don't know God: "Then they asked him, 'Where is your father?' 'You do not know me or my Father,' Jesus replied."[202] Jesus curses the Jews, informing them they are destined to die in sin: "I am going away, and you will look for me, and you will die in your sin. Where I go, you cannot come."[203]

These verses constitute some of the most poisonous attacks on Jews ever written. They would later be used throughout the centuries to justify the most grisly crimes against the Jews. In one of the great ironies and tragedies of history, the editors of the New Testament took a Jewish sage and lover of his people, put a white hood on his head and a swastika on his arm, and sent him out spewing vitriol against his people. The result was a Jesus so altered that he was no longer recognizable as a prince of peace.

Part III

What Christians Have to Learn from the Jewish Jesus

CHAPTER 19

JESUS, LOVER OF ISRAEL

After two thousand years of Christianity, the historical character of Jesus remains shrouded in mystery. Scholars, clergy, and lay-people have used many methods in an effort to unlock the secrets of Christianity's founder. Yet in spite of everything, the most important key has been largely overlooked. Jesus was a Jew, extremely pious and observant.

This secret does not lie in some hidden text lost for millennia, but in the same Christian scriptures that have buried his true nature. A careful examination of these texts reveals the true story of the Jewish Jesus, visible in the most basic Gospel texts before they were altered by Pauline and Lucan editors several decades after Jesus' death.

The Jesus who called Jews a pack of vipers could not be the same man that loved the Jewish people so much he instructed the original twelve apostles, "Do not go among the gentiles or enter any town of the Samaritans. Go rather to the lost sheep of Israel."[204] Eschewing any mission to the non-Jews (that was the later work of Paul), he instructs his disciples to shun the gentiles completely and work only with Jews.

The anti-Semitic Jesus would not have told the Canaanite woman who begged him to exorcize a demon from her daughter: "I was sent only to the lost sheep of Israel…. It is not right to take the children's bread and toss it to the dogs."[205] Likening gentiles to dogs would be consistent with a Jesus who hated the Romans rather than the Jews. Jesus despises the Romans for their cruelty to his people.

He was suspicious of all non-Jews because of how much the Jews had suffered at the hands of foreign invaders. His mission is to redeem the Jews from foreign oppression. He has no time for those outside the community.

The two Jesuses – the anti-Semitic firebrand condemning Jews to hell, and the soft shepherd of Israel with no interest in proselytizing gentiles – are utterly irreconcilable. One is authentic, the other manufactured.

There can be little doubt that Pauline editors changed the story, erasing Rabbi Jesus and inventing Jesus the anti-Semite to substantiate their claim that Jesus came to replace Judaism. Jesus' hatred of his people was a tragic and malevolent fabrication that later justified Christian antipathy toward Jews for rejecting Christianity.

Even opponents of my ideas about Jesus' Jewishness concur on this point. In his book *Answering Jewish Objections to Jesus,* Dr. Michael Brown, the world's leading Jewish-Christian missionary-scholar and my longtime debating adversary, writes, "Our Jewish people have been persecuted, abused, expelled, and even killed for rejecting a counterfeit message of a counterfeit Christ preached by a counterfeit church – and there is blood on the hands of that Church."[206] Dr. Brown insists the message that has been transmitted to us about Jesus is counterfeit, as is the anti-Semitic Church who, up to modern times, identified Jews as their principal enemy. Now that these deeply held beliefs are changing, the genuine Jewish Jesus can be seen anew.

THE JEWISH JESUS

It's important to acknowledge the obvious. I have called into question the veracity of much that is contained in the holy Gospels. I've cast doubt on some of the essential elements of the story of Jesus as they have been handed down by generations of Christians. Obviously, my Christian readers are going to feel somewhat confused or, worse still, offended – which is, of course, not my intention.

Jesus remains the foundational figure of the Christian faith. I am asking my Christian readers to also think of him as a great Jewish patriot and rabbi, who bolstered the Torah's traditions and fought persecution by the Romans. I am asking them to see Jesus as a devout Jew, who loved his people and was ready to die in order to lift from them the oppressive yoke of Rome.

The images may seem inherently contradictory. But then again, it's not so strange to hold two simultaneous and seemingly contradictory views of Jesus. After all, Christian theology itself claims that Jesus was both wholly human and wholly divine, which is also a great contradiction. When Constantine convened the Council of Nicea in 325 CE, the assembled theologians took it upon themselves to determine whether Jesus was man or god. In the end, they refused to compromise on either issue. From then onward, Jesus was believed to be the inextricable synthesis of both. Why then can he not be both the namesake of Christianity and a hero of the Jewish faith?

I do not seek to undermine Christians' belief that Jesus was divine. If he was a great rabbi that fought to free the Jewish people from Roman rule, he is still the same Jesus Christians have treasured for millennia. As a Jew, I cannot embrace Jesus' divinity nor accept that he was the messiah (for reasons I will later explain). But if anything, the new ideas I've introduced can only enhance the respect he should be accorded, not only by Jews but by Christians as well. Why?

Because there is so much Christians have to learn from the Jewish Jesus. Embracing Jesus' Jewishness begins to elucidate his story, his life, his passionate beliefs.

Everywhere we look in the story of Jesus, we find our understanding enriched by a consciousness of Judaism. What was the Garden of Gethsemane? That word, Gethsemane, comes from two Hebrew words, *gat shemenim*, which translate as "olive garden". What was Jesus doing in an olive garden just before he was apprehended by the Roman authorities? He was hiding from the Roman soldiers so he would *not* be apprehended. Who is Mary Magdalene? Mary from Migdal, a Jewish city in the north that exists today in Israel as it did in the ancient Holy Land. What is Caperneum, the city the Gospels refer to so frequently? It's Kfar Nachum, or "Nahum's Village," again in Israel's north. What was the last supper? It was the Passover seder. This is why Jesus and the apostles were drinking wine and eating wafers or "matzo." Wine and unleavened bread would later become the essential vehicles of the Catholic Eucharist, Jesus' metaphorical body and blood, even as they were utterly detached from their Passover origin. These are but a few examples that demonstrate a simple point.

If we introduce new and unfamiliar concepts about Jesus, they need not disturb the religious underpinnings of the Christian faith. *There can be no real understanding of the history and teachings of Jesus if he is divorced from his Jewish roots.*

Jesus' Jewishness is important in that it humanizes Jesus, even for Christians that see him as divine. This is an absolute necessity if people are to learn from his example. "What would Jesus do?" is an irrelevant question if Jesus remains an aloof and perfect deity. If Jesus was divine, then he had no inclination to do evil. Not so for the rest of us humans. We battle dueling impulses at all times. So how could Jesus' supposed behavior have any impact on us? It can't – unless there is a uniquely human dimension to Jesus as well.

This point may be controversial, but it's well worth making. One of the inherent problems of the divinity of Jesus is how *unlike* a divine figure he sometimes acts. The Gospels paint him as a figure that bends to the Romans, ignoring the tyranny of Pontius Pilate, and never inveighing against Rome. If a leader is passive in the face of great evil, he becomes complicit with it. How could Jesus tell his followers to render unto Caesar what is Caesar's? Caesar was a brutal tyrant. To understand Jesus as a Jewish patriot actually enhances his reputation for justice.

My image of Jesus differs a great deal from the received portrait. It makes Jesus a far more praiseworthy figure. He fought tyranny, opposed the Romans, struggled for freedom, and lived righteously and justly with regard to his obligations to his fellow Jews. He was a man who, amid the everyday battles that each of us face, also engaged in the far larger, eternal battle of good against evil. He was a Jewish patriot that gave his life fighting the cruelty of Rome. Ignoring Jesus' Jewishness is tantamount to claiming that Jesus didn't do any of these things. What kind of spiritual leader – or for that matter, moral example – would that make him?

CHAPTER 20

JESUS AGAINST EVIL

Here, then, is the essence of the Jewish Jesus: He was a man whose purpose was defined by his devotion to God's just and righteous law. Even if it meant being tortured and killed for it, Jesus believed God's will as expressed through His law is the reason we're alive. He was courageous, inspired his followers to defend the law, and in the end he paid the ultimate price. At the root of his defense of God's law was Jesus' deep-seated hatred of evil. Christians would do well to heed the subtleties of what Jesus really felt – it remains profoundly relevant to our lives and our world.

Jesus is often remembered for asserting we should love our enemies. Luke quotes him as saying, "But to you who are listening I say: Love your enemies, do good to those who hate you."²⁰⁷ Loving our enemies, though, isn't as simple a matter as it may seem. After all, there are people we dislike, the people with whom we quarrel – and then there are deeper animosities. With reference to the former type, of course, in day-to-day life, you should do your best to love your enemies. How many people do we hate for something petty? The guy who steals your parking space, the work colleague with whom you are competing for a promotion – these are the people we should love, setting aside inconsequential differences.

But Jesus does not tell us to love *God's* enemies. It is one thing to love an irritating colleague, a very different thing to love the murderous Ahmadinejad or Sheikh Hassan Nasrallah, the abominable head of Hezbollah. For Jesus to argue in favor of loving such a man, or any enemy of his people, would be immoral. He neither says nor means anything of the sort.

In the same spirit, Jesus famously exhorted his followers to turn the other cheek. Again, when seen in the context of his life and his purpose, this takes on a meaning that is slightly more complex. Of course, he is certainly right that we should turn the other cheek – to a petty slight. But how can we turn the other cheek to murder or to genocide?

The new picture of Jesus emerging here is one of a hero who was willing to fight against evil. He would never countenance turning the other cheek to allow evil to be victorious against good. Would Jesus tell the Tutsis in Rwanda to turn the other cheek to the Hutus? Would he say such a thing to the Jews about the Nazis? Would he have Blacks in the south turn the other cheek to the Klan? While some might argue that he would, others would say this would make a sham of his teachings. Battling evil is essential to Jesus' self-definition, and we would benefit from learning from his example.

This fact is often overlooked by Christians. The night before he dies, while in the Garden of Gethsemane, the Gospels portray Jesus' conferring with the apostles.

> Then Jesus asked them, "When I sent you without purse, bag, or sandals, did you lack anything?"
>
> "Nothing," they answered.
>
> He said to them, "But now if you have a purse, take it, and also a bag; and if you don't have a sword, sell your cloak and buy one. It is written: 'And he was numbered with the transgressors'; and I tell you that this must be fulfilled in me. Yes, what is written about me is reaching its fulfillment."
>
> The disciples said, "See, Lord, here are two swords."
>
> "That's enough!" he replied.[208]

Jesus expressly asks for swords with which to fight. Yes, there may not have been many – only two in total, to be shared between twelve men. But he wanted to show his followers they must be prepared to resist evil with force. And if they showed that willingness, God would take over from there and fight for them.

He made the same point again even more strongly. From the Book of Matthew: "Do not suppose that I have come to bring peace to the earth. I did not come to bring peace, but a sword. For I have come to turn 'a man against his father, a daughter against her mother, a daughter-in-law against her mother-in-law – a man's enemies will be the members of his own household' (Micah 7:6)."[209]

Jesus was calling his men to arms. An armed insurrection against Rome was his battle cry, even if such armed struggle tore families and communities asunder. Evil has to be resisted.

What he was asserting, and what can inspire us even today, was that faith in God can lead us to victory. It is not man's arms that bring about great victory – even though in this world, man's arms remain necessary as well – but man's attachment to a just and benevolent Creator.

LIVING AS THE MESSIAH

If we but strip away the emendations, revisions, and smears that were added to Jesus' story after his death, then we are able to call his life's purpose as we see it. More than anything else, Jesus believed we can live in a redeemed world.

How do we know this? Jesus believed he was the one that could bring deliverance and salvation to his people. To be sure, someone's intervention was sorely needed. The Jews were suffering so badly under the yoke of Rome. They were in dire need of a redeemer. He concluded that he was the messiah, sent from on high.

As previously explained, claiming to be the messiah is not as controversial as it may seem, nor is messiahship equivalent to divinity. The messiah is a mortal man that will rescue the Jews from political oppression at the hands of their enemies. The messiah is someone that will put an end to the folly of war and cause peace to ensue between nations. But he will be a mortal man, like you and me.

Every American soldier in Afghanistan, to take this one example, can consider himself or herself a redeemer chosen to give women dignity and a people freedom. It's a righteous cause, to be sure. The Taliban are evil men that beat and demean women, stone innocents to death, and live lives of senseless brutality. If you live or act in opposition to such forces, haven't you made a better world?

Moreover, who will fight your battles if you won't do it yourself? Moses' parting of the Red Sea is a key example of the balance between looking to God and looking to ourselves. Moses was up against the might of Egypt. He and his people were fleeing in terror, calling out to God for assistance. God said to Moses: "Why are you crying out to me? Tell the Israelites to move on."[210] This is a powerful passage because it amounts to a statement from God saying: Now is not a time for prayer. Now is the time for action! I will intervene, but I need to see your initiative. Prove you're worthy of My support, and I will grant it to you. And so Moses moved forward, and God acted in kind.

Living as a messiah means you've been called upon. Jesus certainly heard that call, and all of us should live by his example – confronting the world as though God has chosen us as His champion, to redeem mankind from evil. If we all lived in this spirit, it would be a far better world.

CHAPTER 21

TINKERING WITH THE DIVINE

In reading this book, I ask my Christian readers not to discard but to expand their existing ideas about who Jesus really was. But what is the impact of doing so? Does this mean we can't trust the New Testament? Does this mean we're tinkering with a divine document?

Again the answer is no. The writers of the New Testament indeed may have drawn from divine inspiration. Yet, at the same time, they understood the dangers to the Church if they were to antagonize Rome. They witnessed what Rome had done to the Jews, and knew full well that they, too, faced extermination to the last man and woman if the Romans perceived the early Christians to be in league with the Jews in defying Rome. Christians were already being persecuted. Nero used to cover them in tar and flax and light them up like candles, giggling as they burned to death. And this was before the revolt of the year 70. Christians were despised, and the New Testament writers knew it.

We now understand the historical pressures the early Christians were under, from the Jewish revolts to the necessity for winning over Roman converts. Peter's and Paul's intentions aside, the early Christians were in the profoundly unenviable situation of worshipping a dead Jew at a time when anti-Jewish sentiment was reaching a crescendo. It was eternally unfortunate to the relationship between Christians and Jews, as well as to the knowledge of Jesus' true identity, that they modified the documents as they did. At the same time, we can understand their motives – despite their long-term and terrible ramifications for the Jewish people.

I believe the Lucan editors made their changes for the reasons enumerated and to hide the subversive details of the revolutionary nature of Jesus. But the changes they made were not total. They didn't erase the entire original meanings; messages may actually have been intentionally encoded into the Gospels, hidden deeply enough to escape notice by Roman authorities, but in such a way that the content remains available to us today.

This isn't without precedent. There are plenty of examples of this phenomenon in the Hebrew Bible. In order to comprehend God's true meaning, we sort through four levels of interpretation. We refer to these layers of analysis with the word "*pardes*," an acrostic that stands for *peshat, remez, drush,* and *sod: peshat* being the simple, straightforward meaning; *remez,* the alluded to meaning of the text; *drush,* the homiletic meaning of the text; and finally, *sod,* the esoteric meaning of the text.

Beyond the simplest reading of the New Testament, just as in the Hebrew Bible, there remain layers and layers hidden from view. We have seen that Jesus himself was trained in light-and-heavy rabbinical reasoning. Is it not likely that his disciples were as well? It's no stretch to posit that the New Testament was written in a style similar to the Jewish texts that preceded it. It is the duty of Christians to dig deeper and reach the truth about Jesus.

However, as they do so, it is inevitable that Christians will wonder: *If the Jewish Jesus is such an inspirational figure, why can't Jews embrace him as we do?* A variation of this question has been at the crux of the conflict between Christians and Jews for millennia, and the following chapters will attempt to put that question to rest.

PART IV

WHY THE JEWS CANNOT ACCEPT JESUS

CHAPTER 22

THE WORLD'S MOST SUCCESSFUL IDEA

Christianity is the most successful idea in the history of the world. No religion, philosophy, or way of life has ever had more adherents. But its central figure was a Jew, a man who curiously remains estranged from his people in the most serious way until this very day. Once Jesus is stripped of his anti-Semitic cloak and restored as the wise rabbi and devoted Jewish patriot he was, there is much Jews can learn from him. But the Jews have not and cannot ever accept Jesus as he exists in Christian theology.

I say this not to offend Christian believers, nor to dissuade adherents from living a Christian life. On the contrary, I respect and applaud the achievements of Christianity, a religion that has brought billions of people to God. Christians operate the world's largest network of hospitals, orphanages, and schools. The scale of their good deeds in contemporary society is staggering. It is a religion that, as the great Jewish philosopher Maimonides said, has brought the knowledge of God to distant shores and distant lands.[211] Christianity has an incredible power to engender compassionate and pious followers.

God is the one great truth. Judaism, Christianity, and Islam are paths that bring us to Him. One finds God through personal discovery usually directed by the faith in which one is reared, practiced by one's ancestors. The merit of any religion is established not by a test of its theological claims but by the goodness of its followers. Therefore, any religion that leads to a good and Godly life has authenticity and truth, even if we cannot embrace all of its theological claims.

As a Jew I do not believe that Joseph Smith discovered golden plates written in Reformed Egyptian in 1823, which he translated with seer stones. But having had extensive exposure to the strong families and charitable communities that the Mormon Church has built worldwide, I do believe that in Western New York where he claimed to have found the plates, Smith encountered universal religious truths that were incorporated into Mormonism and that account for the high ethical standards of his followers. (The reverse is also true. When a religious figure, such as a Crusader or a terrorist of any religion, devotes his life not to compassionate acts but to a blood-filled apocalypse, it is either he himself or his religion that is fraudulent.)

My intention in this section, where I spell out why Jews reject the Christian Jesus, is not to disparage Christianity but to encourage an understanding of why worship of a man as deity, or belief in a messiah who did not fulfill the messianic prophecies, is anathema to us Jews, a fact that will never change. If we are to move past millennia of anti-Semitism and use the personage of Jesus as a bridge rather than a wedge between Christians and Jews, we must address the meaning of Jesus from all angles and to all observers, Jewish and Christian alike. This will, in turn, set the stage for the discovery of a Jesus Jews can identify with and embrace.

It is to the Jewish perspective of Jesus that we must now turn.

CHAPTER 23

WHY JEWS CANNOT BELIEVE IN THE
DIVINITY AND MESSIAHSHIP OF JESUS

In the centuries after his death, the image and meaning of Jesus changed almost unrecognizably. Gone is the Jesus that lived and preached in Galilee two millennia ago. We have explored how the idea of Jesus evolved during the years following his crucifixion: how the Great Revolt of 66–70 CE poisoned the feelings of gentiles toward Jews; how Peter and Paul seized the opportunity to transform Jesus from a political to a religious rebel; and how the anti-Semitic animus edited into the New Testament wreaked havoc on Judeo-Christian civilization for centuries. But these are all historical dimensions. We need to address a question very much a part of the present.

Why is it that Jews reject the messiahship and divinity of Jesus? We no longer live in an era of Roman savagery and Jewish revolts. Anti-Semitism in Christian lands, at least compared to its prevalence throughout history, is largely in retreat. Why then, in these comparatively enlightened times, do Jews *still* resist the pull of Christianity? Is it Christianity's evangelizing method? Its claims to efface Jewish law and the Abrahamic covenant? Its culture of divine-human sacrifice and repentance? Fixation on the otherworldly? Unstinting insistence on uniformity?

To be blunt, there are more reasons than can be adequately contained in this book. But for now, let's begin with two fundamental sticking points that most directly bar Jews from accepting Jesus – the twin axioms on which Christianity is founded: Jesus' divinity and his messiahship.

CHAPTER 24

DIVINITY

In today's Christian practice, Jesus is worshipped as a divine figure. He is the second part of the Christian Trinity, the son of God, and God the son.

Christian theologians have long seen Jesus' divinity as a crucial element in the arc of all human history. When Adam and Eve ate the fruit of the tree of knowledge in the Garden of Eden, they brought humankind down from a lofty spiritual existence and tied us up in corruption and sin. Man became not only capable of sin, but doomed to it in perpetuity. This original sin of Adam and Eve was bequeathed to all their descendants for all time.

For millennia, mankind was damned to hell for this inheritance. The sin of humanity was so great it required an unequaled sacrifice to atone for it. The sacrifice had to be divine. Therefore, God embodied his word in the person of Jesus through Mary, a Jewish virgin. Jesus' conception was immaculate, so that the son of God could be born without the taint of Adam's sin.

In the Christian telling of this story, when Jesus reached adulthood he spoke out strongly against the Jewish religious leadership, criticizing the Jews for abandoning God's ways. The Jewish leaders prompted the Roman procurator Pontius Pilate to crucify Jesus for treason against Rome. With his death on the cross, Jesus atoned for all mankind, in his generation and every generation, reopening the gates of heaven closed by Adam's sin.

However, as a deity, Jesus could not remain dead. After three days entombed in a cave, he ascended to heaven to take his place as the second part of the Christian godhead.

There are myriad reasons why Jews object to this Christian conception of a divine Jesus. They could fill volumes. Instead, I present only the primary ones: Jews can never worship a man-god; the very idea of a virgin birth is problematic; and God cannot be divided among multiple beings. At the heart of all of these concepts is an even more fundamental disconnect – the clash between Judaism and paganism.

CHAPTER 25

JUDAISM AND PAGANISM

The Jewish faith has stood for millennia as both a monument to monotheism and antidote to paganism. From the very start, the Jews renounced the pantheons of gods the pagans favored, as well as the idea of the demigod, or man-god. Abraham, founding patriarch of the Jews, long ago challenged the self-declared man-god Nimrod, and nearly paid with his life for his rebelliousness. The Midrash, a collection of Jewish legends from the Talmudic sages, relates that as a young boy, Abraham smashed the idols in his father's workshop. For this, Nimrod, the king of Babylon who had declared himself a deity, had Abraham thrown into a furnace. Only through a miracle did Abraham survive the heat of the flames.

Jews, including Jesus, have always found the deification of human beings to be utterly anathema to Judaism. The belief that God can be human is the ultimate heresy. The chasm separating God and man is infinite and unbridgeable.

Moses admonishes the Jewish people: "You saw no form of any kind the day the Lord spoke to you at Horeb out of the fire. Therefore watch yourselves very carefully, so that you do not become corrupt and make for yourselves an idol, an image of any shape, whether formed like a man or a woman."[212]

Much later, the prophet Samuel tells King Saul he will no longer reign over Israel. Samuel says, "He who is the Glory of Israel does not lie or change His mind; for He is not a human being that He should change His mind."[213] The biblical text couldn't be clearer:

God is not a man. He is not human. For Jews, this verse alone ends the debate. Case closed.

This prohibition against deifying any human being is so important it was established as the second of the Ten Commandments. God declares, "You shall have no other gods before Me. You shall not make for yourself an image in the form of anything in heaven above or on the earth beneath or in the waters below."[214]

The Bible is unequivocal. God cannot be human.

There are a multitude of common-sense reasons why God cannot be a living person as well. If we begin to think of God in such a way, His identity becomes unstable. If God is a man, then He must have physical, human qualities. He must have race and gender, establishing a false precedent in creation. If God was indeed a white, Jewish male that roamed the Galilee in the first century CE, then that would effectively diminish women, non-Jews, and people of color as being less Godly. This would stand in direct violation of the biblical doctrine that God created all human beings equally in His image.

God must identify with all people, of all races, religions, and genders. No one deserves to be disenfranchised by a theology that identifies Him with finite, human attributes. God has not anthropomorphic features. He has no body. He is neither born nor grows old. He has no point of origin and He has no end. He cannot be conceived and He cannot die.

No human is infinite, not even Elijah, who ascended to heaven in a fiery chariot and is said never to have died. Elijah's longevity is not intrinsic to him but is rather sustained by God's grace. People have limits in all their capacities. God does not. His omnipotence and omniscience are not threatened by the physical constraints of a mortal body. By putting God into the body of a man, God is reduced to the level of the finite world.

Simply put, for Jews to call Jesus divine is deeply blasphemous. There is an unquantifiable chasm separating God and man. The

Jewish answer to Jesus' or any other man's supposed divinity is clear: it is simply not possible and contradicts the very fundamentals of the Bible and of Judaism.

Judaism is a religion grounded in rationality, and while sometimes it is supra-rational – going beyond human logic – it is never *irrational*, contradicting logic. A finite human cannot be infinite. The two concepts are as deeply contradictory as Judaism and paganism.

CHAPTER 26

THE VIRGIN BIRTH

Many Christians may be surprised to learn the very idea of a virgin birth is as rooted in pagan belief as the concept of the man-god. Christianity's adoption of this element of Jesus' biography is likely the result of Paul's efforts to make the burgeoning religion more palatable to pagan gentiles.

By Jesus' lifetime, virgin birth was not a new idea. In a number of ancient civilizations, deities were commonly born of virgins. According to Hindu beliefs, princess Devaki gave birth to Krishna, an incarnation of Vishnu, without being impregnated by her husband. Instead, his fetus was mystically transferred into her.

There are many stories in Greek mythology as well; most concern Zeus impregnating women. Zeus came down in a shower of gold and impregnated Danae imprisoned in a bronze underground chamber. Other children of Zeus and a mortal woman include Hercules, the Graces, Castor, Pollux, Helen, and Dionysus.

This idea of a deity impregnating a woman had become very popular in the ancient world. Little surprise then that it would have been favored by those seeking to make the Jewish leader Jesus more appealing to ancient pagan sensibilities.

Nevertheless, the notion that God would impregnate a woman is utterly unacceptable for Jews. God is *not* corporeal. As has been made clear, He is not a man. He has no physical characteristics, or a body for that matter. Moreover, He does not engage in relations with a mortal woman. It is unthinkable.

Setting aside the issue of why God would desire to impregnate a mortal woman, there's little question as to why the early Christians thought it necessary to promote the idea. In Christian theology, sex is considered a carnal act profoundly lacking in Godly character. In order to be a proper son of God, Jesus had to be born in the absence of the sexual act. This is, by the way, not the sticking point for Judaism that it is for Christianity. Judaism does not believe sex to be in any way unholy – as readers of my book *Kosher Sex* are profoundly aware. Indeed, the Bible has no word for sex other than "knowledge," connoting the incomparable level of intimacy it establishes between husband and wife.

Furthermore, God would never cause the long-awaited messiah to be born in shame. The Book of Matthew reveals that Mary's husband Joseph knew the child was not his.[215] That left him two options: he could either lie, telling people the child was his own, or else deny he had fathered the boy. Regardless, no one (in his time at least) would ever have believed that God had fathered the child. Although Mary could tell everyone that God impregnated her and she had not been unfaithful, it would understandably have been dismissed as ludicrous by most. The public would only see Jesus as a child fathered by someone other than Mary's husband. Everyone would view the messiah as illegitimate.

This would have been an inauspicious beginning for the life of the Christian Jesus, to say the least.

If we only scratch the surface of the story of Jesus' conception, we begin to find little niggling details that suggest changes have been made to it. For instance, the first chapter of Matthew explains Jesus' conception:

> An angel of the Lord appeared to him in a dream and said, "Joseph son of David, do not be afraid to take Mary home as your wife, because what is conceived in her is from the

Holy Spirit. She will give birth to a son, and you are to give him the name Jesus, because he will save his people from their sins." All this took place to fulfill what the Lord had said through the prophet: "The virgin will conceive and give birth to a son, and they will call him Immanuel" (which means "God with us").[216]

Here, the angel quotes the Hebrew prophet Isaiah in his message to Ahaz, the king of Israel who died in 727 BCE. Yet, oddly for an angel, he misquotes the prophet. The precise and accurate Judaica Press translation of the verse in Isaiah differs from the way it is translated in Matthew. "Therefore, the Lord, of His own, shall give you a sign; behold, the *young woman* is with child, and she shall bear a son, and she shall call his name Immanuel."[217] In Matthew, the angel adds the word *they* to indicate that someone beside the mother is naming the child, suggesting the child will have followers that will attribute God's presence among them to the presence of the child.

The Hebrew word used in the original text, *almah*, as anyone with cursory understanding of Hebrew can attest, means not "virgin" but "young woman." It is derived from the root *alam* or "young." Although a young woman has the potential to be a virgin, the word *almah* does not inherently indicate one way or the other.

In fact a verse in Proverbs uses the word *almah* to refer to a girl that is definitely not a virgin. King Solomon discusses four things: "the way of an eagle in the sky, the way of a snake on a rock, the way of a ship on the high seas, and the way of a man with a young woman [an *almah*]."[218] Their common characteristic? Each of the four leaves no trace. The next verse continues, "This is the way of an adulterous woman: She eats and wipes her mouth and says, 'I've done nothing wrong.'" Solomon is lamenting the adulterous woman who gets away with infidelity since, because she is not a virgin, there is no proof whether or not she engaged in illicit sex.

In addition to the mistranslation, there is a timeframe problem as well. As noted, Ahaz, the King of Israel, was about to go war. He asks the prophet Isaiah for a sign he will be victorious. Isaiah responds there will indeed be a sign. A young woman that seems too young to conceive will have a child. That will prove to you God is with you, hence the name Immanuel. Note that Ahaz died seven centuries before Jesus was born. Is it not impossible for Ahaz to receive a sign hundreds of years after his death? But according to the Christian mistranslation God is saying: *You want proof you're going to win the war? Okay. In seven hundred years' time, when this battle is over and you and everyone you know are nothing but bones in a grave, a virgin is going to have a baby. That is your sign now that you're going to win the war.* Obviously, this is ridiculous.

Equally confusing, how could a virgin having a baby be a sign? Who would even know? As Immanuel Schochet asks, was Mary going to walk around with a gynecological certificate proving her virginity? What proof would there be? Only if the verse means "young maiden" – a woman too young to have a child – does the prophecy make sense.

Again, Gospel editors largely ignorant of Jewish scripture were forced to read the Hebrew Bible in Greek. The Septuagint uses the same word for "young woman" and "virgin," while the Hebrew original uses two distinct terms. The New Testament authors thought Isaiah foretold the birth of a child from a virgin and applied his prophecy to Jesus. Thus, a cardinal principle of Christianity is derived from a Greek already-suspect rending of the Hebrew Bible.

I caution again, this is not to denigrate or deny Christian doctrine. Yet Immaculate Conception is another reason why Jews cannot consider Jesus divine. Just as a man can't be a God, a woman can't have God's child. An unlimited God with no beginning and no end cannot have His origin in the womb of a human female, and He cannot be terminated on a cross.

CHAPTER 27

SPLITTING UP DIVINITY

At the heart of Judaism is its emphasis on monotheism – on the essential oneness and indivisibility of God. Judaism is uncompromising in its reliance on God's unitary nature. He cannot be a man, nor can He be divided up or diminished in any way.

Christianity holds that Jesus is not only both wholly human and wholly divine, he's also one-third of the Holy Trinity, the other two parts of which are God Himself and the Holy Spirit. This *mysterium tremendum* of the Trinity is not compatible with Judaism. Based as it is on a proud tradition of rationalism, Jewish theology cannot embrace the mysterious division of God into three parts.

For Judaism, there are no internal distinctions within God. The *Shema*, the quintessential statement of Jewish belief and the first verse of scripture Jewish children learn to read, says, "Hear O Israel: The Lord our God, the Lord is one."[219] The Bible's position on the indivisible unity of God is therefore clear. Kabbalists refer to God's essence as indivisible, with no separation between elements of God. It is an axiom of the faith that God is an all-encompassing unity. He has no component parts. He will be what He will be.

Nor should there be any intermediary between man and God. The Christian, particularly Catholic, idea that prayer need be directed through an intermediary poses another problem. The principle of an intermediary with God comes from a statement Jesus makes in John: "No one comes to the Father except through me."[220] From this idea stems the most central of all Christian tenets, the idea that belief in Christ alone can provide salvation.

The 1551 Council of Trent cites a similar verse as the source of the doctrine of penance. Just a few chapters after making that statement, John writes, "Again Jesus said, 'Peace be with you! As the Father has sent me, I am sending you.' And with that he breathed on them and said, 'Receive the Holy Spirit. If you forgive anyone's sins, their sins are forgiven; if you do not forgive them, they are not forgiven.'"[221] Penance, now called confession, is a ritual that must take place through a priest. Other doctrines that resulted from such quotations include the notion that saints can intercede with God on people's behalf. The result, after centuries of proliferation and development, is a God many layers distant from the faithful, and a caste of men and women that act as the intermediaries between the divine and ordinary people.

Judaism resoundingly denies the idea that people need an intermediary between themselves and God. The Psalmist says, "The Lord is near to all who call on Him."[222] And, God himself pronounces in the Ten Commandments, "You shall have no other gods before Me."[223] The human relationship with God is direct and immediate.

There is no escaping the finality of these statements. For Jews, it is forbidden to establish a mediator between God and man, and it is unthinkable to conceive of a God split into multiple beings. Every human approaches God directly – and the God they approach is one and the same: infinite, omnipotent, and indivisible.

CHAPTER 28

ORIGINAL SIN

There is one more point key both to Jews' inability to accept Jesus and the essence of Judaism's worldview. This has to do with Jesus' martyrdom.

One of the most famous passages in the New Testament is John 3:16 – "For God so loved the world that He gave His one and only son, that whoever believes in Him shall not perish but have eternal life."[224] This passage is vital to the mechanism of sin and redemption essential to Christianity.

According to Christian doctrine codified by Paul, all men and women are born sinful. Being descended from Adam, who sinned by eating from the tree of knowledge, there is no way for humans to wipe away sin. In fact, all human efforts at self-redemption through repentance and good behavior are doomed to futility.

The nature of that original sin has been subject to fierce and protracted debate. The ancient Manicheans, led by their prophet Mani in the second century CE, took the idea of original sin to its logical extreme, believing the sex act itself to be the introduction of sinfulness into humankind. Although this was ultimately deemed heretical, St. Augustine retained elements of this idea by insisting original sin was preserved and passed forward via intercourse. In his words, "The carnal concupiscence [or rather, sex]…is the daughter of sin, as it were; and whenever it yields assent to the commission of shameful deeds, it becomes also the mother of many sins. Now from this concupiscence whatever comes into being by natural birth is bound by original sin, unless, indeed, it be born again in Him whom the Virgin conceived."[225] In short, only Jesus was free of original sin, thanks to his virgin birth. Everyone else bears the shame, and there's nothing they can do about it. The only solution is to have faith in Jesus, and let his self-sacrifice absolve them.

In Paul's own words, "But when the kindness and love of God our Savior appeared, He saved us, not because of righteous things we had done, but because of His mercy. He saved us through the washing of rebirth and renewal by the Holy Spirit, whom He poured out on us generously through Jesus Christ our Savior, so that, having been justified by His grace, we might become heirs having the hope of eternal life."[226] Simply put, Paul believed all humans are judged by God upon their death, and because all humans are inherently sinful, they are all to be condemned. Only the self-sacrifice of Jesus can "justify" them, wiping away their sins.

It's important to stress this point: Only faith in Jesus admits a human being to heaven. No matter how good a person may be, if he or she fails to accept the divinity and messiahship of Jesus, he or she is damned for all eternity.

This is inadmissible for Jews. Judaism teaches the actions people take are more important than the way they feel, what they think, or what they believe. Almost every law in the Bible governs not faith, but *action*. Jewish law informs Jews what they should eat, what they should wear, and how they should speak. Almost no law has anything to do with how a Jew should feel or believe, with the notable exception of the First Commandment establishing the primacy of God and our need to love Him.

In contrast, Christian theology holds that actions mean nothing unless accompanied by faith in Jesus and his sacrifice. This defies Jewish belief that deeds are more important than thoughts, and action more important than dogma.

It also defies our experience of life itself. Those of us who have experienced marriage, for example, know the institution is not built on the love we have in our heart but on the loving *actions* we practice with our hands. A means-tested, performance-centered religion like Judaism can't align with a school of thought that holds faith, martyrdom, and justification in the afterlife are more important than the here and now.

It is inhumane to hold someone accountable for the sins of another. Judaism believes in a just God that holds people responsible as individuals and doesn't punish them for their ancestors' sins. In Deuteronomy, Moses says "Parents are not to be put to death for their children, nor children put to death for their parents; each will die for their own sin."[227]

Ezekiel prophesies about a son who witnesses his father's sins and withholds from duplicating the same behavior. God says of that person, "He will not die for his father's sin; he will surely live."[228] The prophet continues: "Yet you ask, 'Why does the son not share the guilt of his father?' Since the son has done what is just and right and has been careful to keep all My decrees, he will surely live. The one who sins is the one who will die. The child will not share the guilt of the parent, nor will the parent share the guilt of the child. The righteousness of the righteous will be credited to them, and the wickedness of the wicked will be charged against them.[229]

The matter is settled by God's own pronouncement. No person inherits or is punished for someone else's sin.

Judaism is predicated on the belief that each of us is born neither good nor bad, but innocent. It is our actions and our actions alone that will determine whether we are righteous or wicked.

How would you view a judge that sentences a twenty-five-year-old innocent man to the electric chair because his father murdered a child on a playground? How could we believe God Himself would be guilty of monstrous violations of simple justice? How could we believe God would condemn every last innocent individual that has done nothing wrong to anyone, just because he or she was a Buddhist or a Jew? I have to ask my beloved Evangelical Christian brothers and sisters, is Gandhi really in hell forever because he was a Hindu? And if so, can we possibly call God just?

What makes this question more urgent is that Christians believe strongly in personal accountability, that people can pull themselves up by their bootstraps. Yet they are endorsing a theology that states precisely the opposite. Like a child born into poverty who may later claim that his poor station in life justified his inability to make something more of his life, so, too, we are all born in sin and can do nothing to better our spiritual station other than to repose faith in Jesus. There is nothing we can do to elevate our circumstances. No action on earth can make us virtuous. Rather, we need to be plucked out of sin by placing all hope in Jesus. Redemption is not something we can achieve on our own.

Judaism cannot accept this. It holds all are born innocent, all are accountable to God for their behavior – no excuses. We have a conscience. We are expected to know right from wrong. We will be judged by one thing and one thing alone: our actions. Will they be righteous or wicked? No child will ever be punished for something he did not do or the action of a forebear. God, it turns out, is just.

CHAPTER 29

SALVATION AND REPENTANCE

Setting aside the question of original sin, the sacrifice of Jesus is also fraught with problems for Jews. Paul believed Jesus' martyrdom was the cure-all for Christianity, saving the human race in one monumental stroke. However, the Bible tells us specifically that the blood of a sacrifice cannot atone for an intentional sin.

In the fourth chapter of Leviticus, God tells Moses that animal offerings can be made "when anyone sins unintentionally and does what is forbidden in any of the Lord's commands."[230] The fact that the sin is *unintentional* gets special emphasis. The text of Leviticus continues: "If the whole Israelite community sins unintentionally and does what is forbidden in any of the Lord's commands, even though the community is unaware of the matter, when they realize their guilt, and the sin they committed becomes known, the assembly must bring a young bull as a sin offering and present it before the tent of meeting."[231] Later there are two more references: "When a leader sins unintentionally and does what is forbidden... he must bring as his offering a male goat without defect,"[232] and "If any member of the community sins unintentionally...they must bring as their offering for the sin they committed a female goat without defect."[233] The point is not to be missed: sacrifices are designed primarily to atone for unintentional sin.

The only thing that can save us from the consequences of *intentional* sin is repentance. The Hebrew Bible's most famous story of repentance concerns Jonah and the whale. Jonah has been sent to

Nineveh to preach to the people and steer them away from wickedness. After being swallowed by a whale and vomited up, Jonah takes to the streets of Nineveh proclaiming, "Forty more days and Nineveh will be overthrown."[234]

The Ninevites take heed. Their king issues an emergency decree, "Let everyone call urgently on God. Let them give up their evil ways and their violence. Who knows? God may yet relent and with compassion turn from His fierce anger so that we will not perish."[235] Without an animal sacrifice in sight, God listens and indeed relents. The people and leadership of the city took their fate into their own hands, and by doing so, they repented and saved themselves.

"When God saw what they did and how they turned from their evil ways, He relented and did not bring on them the destruction he had threatened."[236] Here, in the most celebrated story of sin and repentance in the entire Bible, there is absolutely no mention of any animal sacrifice or blood. Rather, forgiveness hinges on a change of the human heart.

So what are Jews to make of Christian theology that dictates the sacrifice of Jesus is all that is needed to atone for even the most serious intentional sins? More problematic, God says explicitly and repeatedly that He hates *human* sacrifice. God tells the Jewish people in no uncertain terms not to engage in the idolatry of the Canaanites. He explains Canaanite practices are an abomination. "You must not worship the Lord your God in their way, because in worshipping their gods, they do all kinds of detestable things the Lord hates. They even burn their sons and daughters in the fire as sacrifices to their gods."[237]

God reiterates this point in Ezekiel. "And you took your sons and daughters whom you bore to Me and sacrificed them as food to the idols. Was your prostitution not enough? You slaughtered My children and sacrificed them to the idols."[238] If God has this to say about the sacrificing of children, how can a Jew be expected to believe that God would sacrifice a child of His own?

BLOOD SACRIFICE AND THE TEMPLE

Some Christian theologians have suggested Jesus' sacrifice is intended to replace all blood sacrifices that came before. According to this line of thinking, the blood of Jesus makes up for the absence of Judaism's Temple in Jerusalem. But, as I've explained, Judaism does not tolerate blood sacrifice for any intentional sin, nor does it allow for human sacrifice.

There are deeper and more fundamental issues within this idea for us to explore. According to Leviticus, blood sacrifice had to occur in the Temple, and nowhere else. The text itself reads, "For the life of a creature is in the blood, and I have given it to you to make atonement for yourselves *on the altar*; it is the blood that makes atonement for one's life."[239] It says "on the altar," referring to the First Temple, which was destroyed in 586 BCE. The Second Temple was built in 516 BCE, and there was no Temple standing for the seventy years in between. If, as Christian theologians suggest, Jesus' blood was essential for atonement in lieu of these Temple sacrifices, he came approximately five hundred years too late.

Some may protest that this suggestion refers to the destruction of the Second Temple, which, as we've seen, occurred at the end of the Jewish Revolt in 70 BCE. That would have Jesus' blood supplanting sacrifices that should have occurred in the decades after his death. The trouble is this doesn't accord with established prophecy.

The prophet Ezekiel makes it clear sacrifices will resume with the rebuilding of the Third Temple. He describes the Third Temple, including a room for preparing sacrifices: "A room with a doorway was by the portico in each of the inner gateways, where the burnt offerings were washed. In the portico of the gateway were two tables on each side, on which the burnt offerings, sin offerings, and guilt offerings were slaughtered."[240]

A few chapters later, Ezekiel explains what will be sacrificed on the altar in the Third Temple.

> You are to give a young bull as a sin offering to the priests.... You are to take some of its blood and put it on the four horns of the altar and on the four corners of the upper ledge and all around the rim, and so purify the altar and make atonement for it. You are to take the bull for the sin offering and burn it in the designated part of the Temple area outside the sanctuary. On the second day you are to offer a male goat without defect for a sin offering, and the altar is to be purified as it was purified with the bull.... You are to offer a young bull and a ram from the flock, both without defect.... For the seven days you are to provide a male goat daily for a sin offering; you are also to provide a young bull and a ram from the flock, both without defect. For seven days they are to make atonement for the altar and cleanse it; thus they will dedicate it. At the end of these days, from the eighth day on, the priests are to present your burnt offerings and fellowship offerings on the altar.[241]

In Ezekiel's description of sacrificial rites in the Third Temple yet to come, there is no mention of Jesus or his blood playing any part. Clearly, once the Third Temple comes to be, sacrificial practice will return to the ways of the era of the First Temple. Thus, even if we were to accept Christian theologians' claim that Jesus' martyrdom replaced sacrifices in the absence of the Second Temple, this sacrifice would be eclipsed by the Third Temple – in a stroke, instantly making Christianity obsolete.

Judaism is bolstered by a tradition applicable in any world environment because of its fundamental truth and simplicity. Judaism neither believes that sacrifice is a sufficient way for people to atone, nor does it accept that original sin can be applied to the human race en masse. Our sins are ours alone to repent for.

When some Jews rebel against Moses, God sends a plague to afflict the Jewish people. Aaron stops the plague with an incense offering; no blood is involved: "But Aaron offered the incense and made atonement for them."[242] And in the fifth chapter of Amos, the prophet disparages those who think sacrifice alone will atone for their misdeeds. "I hate, I despise your religious festivals; your assemblies are a stench to me. Even though you bring me burnt offerings and grain offerings, I will not accept them."[243]

God criticizes the Jews again through Jeremiah when they rely too heavily on sacrificial law, ignoring the rest of the Torah and the sincerity of repentance. "For when I brought your ancestors out of Egypt and spoke to them, I did not just give them commands about burnt offerings and sacrifices, but I gave them this command: Obey Me, and I will be your God and you will be My people. Walk in obedience to all I command you, that it may go well with you."[244]

God explicitly says confession is the primary means by which people can receive atonement. When one person harms another, they "must confess the sin they have committed.[245] Blood does not ameliorate the sin; confession and personal resolve to improve future actions are what the Torah demands of sinners.

Prayer is instrumental in seeking forgiveness from God, as God tells Solomon after he finishes dedicating the Temple. God says, "If My people, who are called by My name, will humble themselves and pray and seek My face and turn from their wicked ways, then will I hear from heaven, and I will forgive their sin."[246]

In Psalms, King David reinforces the idea that sacrifices are not the key to repentance: "Sacrifice and offering You did not desire, but my ears You have opened; burnt offerings and sin offerings You did not require."[247]

In many of my debates with Dr. Michael Brown, he says only the blood of Christ will atone for my sins, as there is no Temple today and no animal sacrifice. "Only the death of Jesus and accepting him into my heart will bring salvation" is the common refrain from my many Christian readers. Their good intentions aside, the mistake they make is in believing that the Bible prescribed only one method of atonement for sin, namely blood and animal sacrifice.

What is in fact clear from the Bible in general, and the Book of Leviticus in particular, is that animal sacrifice and the sprinkling of blood was only one of several methods by which people achieved atonement. For example, the Bible states any person that could not afford to bring an animal sacrifice to the Temple had alternate paths to forgiveness. While the Book of Leviticus first cites a lamb as an ideal offering, it continues, "Anyone who cannot afford a lamb is to bring two doves or two young pigeons to the Lord as a penalty for their sin."[248] If even that is too dear, then one need not sacrifice an animal at all: "If, however, they cannot afford two doves or two young pigeons, they are to bring as an offering for their sin a tenth of an ephah of the finest flour for a sin offering."[249] Flour, not blood. So clearly, it was possible to repent at the Temple without spilling blood of any kind.

While it is true that sacrifice in the Temple was an element of the atonement process in ancient times, Jesus was not needed as its replacement. In fact, the prophet Hosea says clearly prayer is to be the substitute for sacrifice. In speaking about the Jewish people during their exile, he says, "Take words with you and return to the Lord. Say to Him: 'Forgive all our sins and receive us graciously, that we may offer the fruit of our lips.'"[250] Jews are to use prayer in the absence of the Temple, and thus seek forgiveness from God.

Ethical behavior is by far the better tool with which to receive repentance. As Proverbs says, "To do what is right and just is more acceptable to the Lord than sacrifice."[251]

CHAPTER 30

A DAVIDIC MESSIAH?

But what of Jesus' messiahship? This may turn out to be the most important question of all.

The Bible is exceedingly clear that the messiah must hail from the House of David. This idea is explicitly repeated often and with great consistency in the statements of the Hebrew prophets. For example: "A shoot will come up from the stump of Jesse; from his roots a branch will bear fruit. The Spirit of the Lord will rest on him – the Spirit of wisdom and of understanding, the Spirit of counsel and of might, the Spirit of knowledge and fear of the Lord."[252] And, "'The days are coming,' declares the Lord, 'when I will raise up for David a righteous branch, a king who will reign wisely and do what is just and right in the land.'"[253]

It's striking, then, that the Gospels explain that Jesus was not from David's house, nor a male descendant of any but God, as he was born of a virgin. I've already explained it is anathema to Judaism for the divine to be in any way mortal or otherwise individuated as a human man. But if we set this stricture aside and take the Gospels at face value, already it seems they have contradicted the prophecies.

Some Christians have explained that Mary was from the bloodline of King David,[254] but the Gospels of Matthew and Luke both specifically trace Jesus' genealogy to David through Joseph. Not only that, even if Mary was descended from David, Jewish law traces genealogy paternally. Jesus still would not qualify as the messiah, at least by the standard set by the prophecies he was supposed to fulfill.

Matters are further complicated by the fact that the genealogies
in Matthew and Luke contradict one another. They even disagree regarding which branch of David's descendants Jesus came from. Matthew says he was from Solomon's line:

> This is the genealogy of Jesus the Messiah the son of David,
> the son of Abraham:
>> Abraham was the father of Isaac,
>> Isaac the father of Jacob,
>> Jacob the father of Judah and his brothers,
>> Judah the father of Perez and Zerah, whose mother
>> was Tamar,
>> Perez the father of Hezron,
>> Hezron the father of Ram,
>> Ram the father of Amminadab,
>> Amminadab the father of Nahshon,
>> Nahshon the father of Salmon,
>> Salmon the father of Boaz, whose mother was Rahab,
>> Boaz the father of Obed, whose mother was Ruth,
>> Obed the father of Jesse,
>> and Jesse the father of King David.
>> *David was the father of Solomon*, whose mother had been
>> Uriah's wife.[255]

Matthew concludes his genealogy by linking David and Solomon
with Jesus: "And Jacob the father of Joseph, the husband of Mary,
and Mary was the mother of Jesus who is called the Messiah."[256]

Luke differs, claiming that Jesus was of Nathan's line:

> Now Jesus himself was about thirty years old when he began
> his ministry. He was the son, so it was thought, of Joseph,
>> the son of Heli, the son of Matthat,
>> the son of Levi, the son of Melki,
>> the son of Jannai, the son of Joseph,

the son of Mattathias, the son of Amos,
the son of Nahum, the son of Esli,
the son of Naggai, the son of Maath,
the son of Mattathias, the son of Semein,
the son of Josech, the son of Joda,
the son of Joanan, the son of Rhesa,
the son of Zerubbabel, the son of Shealtiel,
the son of Neri, the son of Melki,
the son of Addi, the son of Cosam,
the son of Elmadam, the son of Er,
the son of Joshua, the son of Eliezer,
the son of Jorim, the son of Matthat,
the son of Levi, the son of Simeon,
the son of Judah, the son of Joseph,
the son of Jonam, the son of Eliakim,
the son of Melea, the son of Menna,
the son of Mattatha, *the son of Nathan*,
the son of David.[257]

While Christian theologians have attempted to reconcile such differing family trees, either one excludes Jesus from being the messiah.[258]

As God says to David, "But you will have a son who will be a man of peace and rest, and I will give him rest from all his enemies on every side. His name will be *Solomon*, and I will grant Israel peace and quiet during his reign. He is the one who will build a house for My Name. He will be My son, and I will be his Father. And I will establish the throne of his kingdom over Israel forever."[259] This immediately excludes the genealogy found in Luke. If Jesus is descended from David through his son Nathan rather than Solomon, he cannot be the messiah.

Yet even according to the genealogy in Matthew, Jesus ends up excluded. As Matthew writes, he strives to match his record up to a numerological stricture, "Thus there were fourteen generations in all from Abraham to David, fourteen from David to the exile to Babylon, and fourteen from the exile to the Messiah."[260] To make Jesus' ancestors add up, he omits four kings. These are Ahaziah, Joash, Amaziah, and Jehoiakim.[261]

The casual reader's eyes may glaze over at these long lists of names, but a crucial point arises once these four kings are restored to this genealogy. Elsewhere in the Bible it is made clear that Jeconiah is the son of Jehoiakim, as in Jeremiah where it is written, "…when he carried Jehoiachin son of Jehoiakim king of Judah into exile from Jerusalem to Babylon."[262] Sickened by the idolatrous and blasphemous misbehavior of Jeconiah, God curses him and all of his descendents. God specifically vows that "none of his offspring will prosper, none will sit on the throne of David or rule anymore in Judah."[263]

If Jesus was indeed descended from Jeconiah, he is included in the curse and forbidden from being the King Messiah as described in the Hebrew Bible. Both New Testament genealogies therefore disqualify Jesus from being the messiah: Luke because the messiah must come from Solomon, and Matthew because he must not come from Jeconiah.

Furthermore, the messiah's arrival was to be heralded by the prophet Elijah. "See, I will send the prophet Elijah to you before that great and dreadful day of the Lord comes."[264] While there is some speculation in the New Testament that John the Baptist might be Elijah, there is no outside evidence to attest to this. Even the Gospel of John directly refutes this idea. When priests and Levites came from Jerusalem to interrogate John, "They asked him, 'Then who are you? Are you Elijah?' He said, 'I am not.'"[265]

On the basis of the text of the New Testament alone, we can conclude Jesus simply couldn't have been the prophesied messiah. That case is bolstered even further when we look to what he was supposed to accomplish.

CHAPTER 31

JESUS AND THE MESSIANIC PROPHECIES

The most compelling reason for Jews' inability to accept Jesus as the messiah is his failure to fulfill the messianic prophecies as given clearly by the Hebrew biblical prophets. Isaiah's famous messianic prophecy is as follows:

> The wolf will live with the lamb, the leopard will lie down with the goat, the calf and the lion and the yearling together; and a little child will lead them. The cow will feed with the bear, their young will lie down together, and the lion will eat straw like the ox. The infant will play near the cobra's den, and the young child will put its hand into the viper's nest. They will neither harm nor destroy on all My holy mountain, for the earth will be filled with the knowledge of the Lord as the waters cover the sea.[266]

Do we live in a world where peace reigns, war is a distant memory, and disease, hunger, fear, and hatred are all eradicated? If Jesus was truly the messiah Isaiah prophesied, the world would be a very different place. The sad truth is young children are gunned down on city streets for being in the wrong place at the wrong time. We live in an age of fanatical terrorism, war, the death of innocent noncombatants, and the willful and purposeful targeting of innocent civilians by suicide bombers and unrepentant religious murderers. No matter how you stretch the metaphors, this prophecy has still not come to pass.

Jeremiah echoes the message that in the time of the messiah knowledge of God will permeate our world. "No longer will they teach their neighbor, or say to one another, 'Know the Lord,' because they will all know Me, from the least of them to the greatest."[267] I myself have engaged in numerous public and even televised debates with world-renowned atheists, authors of international best sellers that deny God even exists. And in our day, Europe is slowly becoming a continent where God and church attendance are in sharp decline. Clearly, ours is not an age where God-awareness and a Godly moral culture are flourishing.

There is also the famous prophecy that the messiah will end all war: "He will judge between the nations and will settle disputes for many peoples. They will beat their swords into plowshares and their spears into pruning hooks. Nation will not take up sword against nation, nor will they train for war anymore."[268]

This message is repeated by other prophets. Zechariah says the messiah "will proclaim peace to the nations. His rule will extend from sea to sea and from the River to the ends of the earth."[269] In Ezekiel, we learn that in the messianic age, all weapons will be destroyed. "Then those who live in the towns of Israel will go out and use the weapons for fuel and burn them up."[270]

But none of this has come to pass. In the centuries since Jesus, war and violence have abounded on our planet. People kill each other over all kinds of disputes. I would challenge any Christian missionary to tell terror victims in Israel, the families of 9/11, the innocent dead in Rwanda, or those who experienced genocide in Darfur that there is no more war or killing on earth.

Furthermore, Psalms says the messiah will have universal dominion and dominance over his enemies. "In his days may the righteous flourish and prosperity abound till the moon is no more. May he rule from sea to sea and from the River to the ends of the earth. May the desert tribes bow before him and his enemies lick the dust."[271]

In previous generations, Jesus' own followers participated in some of the gravest atrocities in world history. Furthermore, Jesus did not even have dominion over his own land. He was a rebel against colonial overlords that enslaved and brutalized his people. His enemies nailed him to a cross, mocking him all the while, and leaving him on a crucifix to die the long, tortured, and ignominious death of a political dissident. Though his martyrdom had meaning, it was neither the life nor death of the messiah.

Zechariah says that after the messiah has established his dominion, "Then the survivors from all the nations that have attacked Jerusalem will go up year after year to worship the King, the Lord Almighty."[272] The messiah is supposed to bring about the universal conversion of all people either to Judaism or to ethical monotheism, but this clearly has not happened. There are many people in the world today that follow some sort of idolatrous cult even though the messiah was to bring an end to all forms of idolatry: "I will banish the names of the idols from the land, and they will be remembered no more."[273]

The messiah is also supposed to rebuild the Temple. As Ezekiel says, "I will put My sanctuary among them forever. My dwelling place will be with them."[274] Rather than usher in the era of the Third Temple, Jesus' life marked the end of the Second Temple period, and after two millennia, Jews are still without a Temple in Jerusalem.

The biblical messiah is also supposed to initiate an era without death. Isaiah says, "He will swallow up death forever."[275] This is certainly not our global condition nor was it during the lifetime of Jesus. According to Isaiah, the messiah will resurrect the dead. Isaiah says, "But your dead will live, Lord; their bodies will rise. Let those who dwell in the dust, wake up and shout for joy."[276] Ezekiel echoes the same message, "I am going to open your graves and bring you up from them."[277] Again, this is hardly part of the post-Jesus world.

Ezekiel says there will be no world hunger after the messiah comes. It will be a time of super-abundance: "I will call for the grain and make it plentiful and will not bring famine upon you."[278] Ezekiel even explains that during the messianic age there will be a fundamental change in the natural order. As quoted before, the wolf will lie with the lamb. Animals will lose their predatory instinct. Trees will yield fruit every month. "Fruit trees of all kinds will grow on both banks of the river. Their leaves will not wither, nor will their fruit fail. Every month they will bear fruit, because the water from the sanctuary flows to them."[279] However, there is poverty all over the world today, and millions of people, including children, are starving.

The messiah is also prophesied to return all of Israel to Zion. God tells Ezekiel that when the messiah comes, "I will take the Israelites out of the nations where they have gone. I will gather them from all around and bring them back into their own land."[280] Later, Ezekiel even explains how the land will be divided among the Jews in Israel. However, in the era since Jesus, Jews have found themselves more scattered across the globe than ever. And while there is a State of Israel, the Jews must fight tenaciously just to hold on to the land as their enemies encircle it.

In the messianic age, gentiles are to look to Jews for spiritual guidance. "In those days ten people from all languages and nations will take firm hold of one Jew by the hem of his robe and say, 'Let us go with you, because we have heard that God is with you.'"[281] This also is clearly not the case, as since the days of Jesus, when ten men reach out to grab a Jew, it has usually been in the context of a pogrom.

Gentiles will help Jews in military matters: "Foreigners will rebuild your walls, and their kings will serve you."[282] But Mahmoud Ahmadinejad is hardly reaching out to offer Jews assistance, but attempting to aim a nuclear warhead at Israel. The German Nazis helped even less.

Christians, realizing the messianic prophecies remain unfulfilled, claim that Jesus will return in a Second Coming to complete his task. However, nowhere in scripture is there any mention of such an event. To judge by his own statements, Jesus seemed singularly fixated on fulfilling the prophecy within his own lifetime. In Matthew, Jesus says, "This generation will certainly not pass away until all these things have happened,"[283] and in Mark he says, "The kingdom of God has come near."[284] In Luke he says, referring again to the fulfillment of the prophecy, "Look at the fig tree, and all the trees. When they sprout leaves, you can see for yourselves and know that summer is near. Even so, when you see these things happening, you know that the kingdom of God is near."[285]

Elsewhere, in the Book of James, the fulfillment of the prophecy is as close as can be: "You too, be patient and stand firm, because the Lord's coming is near. Don't grumble against one another, brothers and sisters, or you will be judged. The Judge is standing at the door!"[286] Most explicitly of all, Jesus actually says that his followers will see the coming of the messiah themselves, "I say to all of you: From now on you will see the Son of Man sitting at the right hand of the Mighty One and coming on the clouds of heaven."[287]

Later prophecies of such a return may have been intended metaphorically, as they too have not come to pass. The Book of Revelation says that Jesus is coming soon.[288] But it has been two millennia since Revelation was written. In the event that Jesus does return in a second coming, Jews will have to rethink their current position. Until then, there is no justification for Jews' acceptance of Jesus as the messiah.

Yet my Christian brothers and sisters continue to tell me that although Jesus has not fulfilled the messianic prophecies, his messiahship has been validated. He will fulfill them all at the time of his Second Coming. The classic Jewish response to this? We will wait until then to declare him the messiah. But until that happens, there is no reason to believe Jesus is the long-promised redeemer.

CHAPTER 32

AN ETERNAL COVENANT

Did Jesus end the covenant between God and the Jews, forged by Abraham many centuries before? The early Christians argued this was the case. They took it upon themselves to declare an end to the covenant between God and the Jews, replacing it with a new one. For this reason, the Christian Bible is called the New Testament, replacing what they refer to as the "Old," outdated, ossified, discarded Testament.

If this is what accepting Jesus means, then Jews will never be able to do so. Besides the anxiety they will obviously feel when told their religion is no longer valid, it is also contrary to their fundamental self-definition.

Christian thinkers have long insisted Jesus represented the beginning of a new covenant between man and God. As Paul says, "Now that this faith has come, we are no longer under a guardian."[289] In other words, the law no longer applies. However, Judaism maintains the covenant between God and the people of Israel embodied in the Hebrew scriptures is eternally valid and binding, and it is never to be superseded by a new covenant or testament.

God explains His eternal covenant with Abraham and his descendants in Genesis: "I will establish My covenant as an everlasting covenant between Me and you and your descendants after you for the generations to come, to be your God and the God of your descendants after you."[290] This does not sound like a promise with an expiration date.

Indeed, one must ask the question as to whether God is prone to convulsions or is fickle. One day He decides that His law is everlasting, His covenant eternal; the next day He abolishes it completely, saying His laws were never really that important or permanent, and that a new nation has replaced the Jews with a new covenant? And if God changes His covenant so often, then surely He can replace the Christians with, say, the Muslims just as easily, which is indeed what the Muslims, the Mormons, and so many other later groups claim. If anything, the Christian understanding of a God who is so deeply capricious and inconsistent is much more reminiscent of pagan and Greek gods who are prone to temper tantrums than of the eternal God of Israel who transcends all definition.

In subsequent eras, the permanence of God's promise was something all Jews relied on. Toward the end of his life, King David says, "If my house were not right with God, surely he would not have made with me an everlasting covenant, arranged and secured in every part."[291] In Chronicles, David says of God's covenant with the Jewish people, "He confirmed it to Jacob as a decree, to Israel as an everlasting covenant."[292]

Moses himself insists the Jews are to keep the Torah forever. "The secret things belong to the Lord our God, but the revealed things belong to us and to our children forever, that we may follow all the words of this law."[293] God swears the Torah and its laws are forever, applicable at all times and in all situations. If God knew that He would eventually abrogate the laws of the Torah and replace them with a new covenant in Jesus, He would never have stated the Torah is forever.

All the great Jewish leaders and prophets are totally convinced the Torah and God's covenant with Israel are permanent. Even Jesus echoes this point in Matthew: "For truly I tell you, until heaven and earth disappear, not the smallest letter, not the least stroke of a pen, will by any means disappear from the Law until everything is accomplished. Therefore anyone who sets aside one of the least of these commands and teaches others accordingly will be called least in the kingdom of heaven, but whoever practices and teaches these commands will be called great in the kingdom of heaven."[294]

Despite early Christians' efforts to declare the covenant annulled, there's simply no way to reinterpret this overwhelming evidence of God's covenant with the Jews. God's law stands, now and forever. For either Jesus or the editors of the Gospels to claim otherwise is to contradict a fundamental tenant of Judaism. It's just one more reason Jews cannot accept Jesus.

CHAPTER 33

EVANGELIST METHODS

Now that we have addressed the questions of Jesus' divinity, virgin birth, sacrifice, messiahship, and God's eternal covenant, we arrive at the subtler yet no less important disagreements between Judaism and Christianity.

Judaism is more than just a formula for deciding whether or not one accepts Jesus as divine. It is the source of values that define how Jews see the world. And that Jewish viewpoint is incompatible with the evangelical style, the mystical attitude, and the intolerance of diversity that have crept into Christianity.

Here I refer to the methods some Christians have employed to try to win conversions. Missionaries often use emotional arguments, guilt trips, and even scare tactics in an effort to persuade Jews to join the ranks of Christianity. This mindset is similar to that which led early Christians to claim God's covenant with Abraham and the Jewish people had been dispelled. There is a deep-seated desire on the part of some Christians to see Jews convert and confirm that Christianity has indeed replaced Judaism.

Not every branch of Christianity engages in such evangelizing. In fact, many mainstream Christian groups repudiate and condemn these techniques. Joel Osteen received a great deal of flak from some of his Christian supporters when he appeared on Larry King's TV program and was asked point blank whether Jews could go to heaven. Osteen replied, "Here's what the Bible teaches and from the Christian faith this is what I believe. I just think that only God will judge a person's heart." As difficult as this may be for some hard-line evangelists to swallow, Jews readily concur with Osteen. Non-belief in Jesus can't consign righteous Jews or anyone else to an eternity in hell. God is just, and for Him to insist on such draconian punishment is incompatible with His essence.

My good friend the Jewish Christian scholar Dr. Michael Brown is among those evangelists that attempt to ply Jews with fear. "Like it or not, Israel's history suggests that judgment has been the norm... in God's sight, it is not just the Adolph Hitlers of the world who are unrighteous. Rather, by His standards, most human beings (including most Jews) are unrighteous."[295] He blithely states, "As surely as God judged our people [the Jews] in the past for our sins, he will judge us in the future for our sins.... I wonder if you take seriously the intensity and scope of the horrible judgments that have already fallen upon us in the past.... And they will happen again if we follow a similar course of behavior."[296]

Dr. Brown continues: "The Messiah did come to bring peace, but as a people, we [the Jews] missed the opportunity to receive him as our King, and we have been suffering the consequences ever since. Should we fault Jesus, our righteous Prophet and Savior who warned us in advance, or should we fault those of our forefathers who failed to listen to him?"[297]

Aggressive Christian evangelism has a long history. St. Augustine of Hippo framed the need for Christianity by claiming Judaism was just too hard to follow, and people therefore needed another, easier way to achieve salvation.[298] Many missionaries today use stories about finding salvation, experiencing grace, and recognizing Jesus' love as methods to sway non-Christians.

This strategy has never had wide success with Jews. Jews do not feel the need to keep the Torah perfectly; they know people make mistakes. This is the reason God provides for repentance. Jews do not need Jesus' love when they can receive love directly from God and from each other. Jews do not need Christians' personal religious experiences because they have their own from which to grow as individuals and as a people. Therefore, despite centuries of emotional appeals as well as threats, Christians still find themselves in a world with Jews who have not accepted Jesus.

Evangelists also insist God is more vengeful than Jews believe. Again, Dr. Brown: "That *is* the kind of God he will be if you scorn Him and reject His Word. If you choose to go your own way and do your own thing, you *will* suffer His wrath."[299]

Going further, Brown writes, "[You may ask] why do [I] claim that it is only those who believe in Jesus who go to heaven.... It hardly seems fair to say that people will go to hell just because they don't believe the same way you do. That's a good point, and it deserves a good response. Here it is: All of us have sinned, all of us need a savior, and Jesus alone can wipe away our guilt...."[300] Not so. Repentance is what wipes away our guilt, and for the Jews, Jesus has not proven he has anything to do with the process of forgiveness, something dependent solely on the individual's actions.

Brown's and other evangelists' assertions of God's vengefulness do not mean Jews should throw out their own theology. Historically, we have embraced a loving God that wants us to follow the Torah, not any other path. Evangelists' insistence on some other reality is not reason enough for us to abandon our established practices and beliefs. Guilt trips and scare tactics are also doomed to fail. Christians try to make Jews feel bad about not believing in Jesus, and tell us we will go to hell if we do not accept Christianity, as we see clearly in this quote from Dr. Brown, particularly unfortunate in light of 9/11: "We should see them [people that don't accept Jesus] as people about to get on a plane we know will soon crash. It is remotely possible that one or two of the passengers will survive, but for the most part, we can assume that just about everyone who gets on board will soon die. Therefore, we should warn them not to get on that particular flight, urging them to go another way."[301]

Elsewhere Dr. Brown pleads, "Isn't it time for you to put your heavy burden down – your burden of sin, of guilt, of sorrow, of pain, of confusion, of sadness, of alienation, of bitterness, of anger, of doubt, of unbelief, of whatever it is that weighs you down or separates you from God – and take the Messiah's burden instead?"[302] And, "…if you scorn him and reject His Word. If you choose to go your own way and do your own thing, you *will* suffer His wrath."[303]

Even when Brown adds, "There is no question that our responsibility as children of the one true God is to tell everyone that there is a judgment, there is a hell,"[304] Jews remain steadfast. Jews simply do not believe in hell the way that Christians do, and certainly do not focus on it anywhere near as much. Jews have the avenue of repentance to remove their guilt, without any requirement for acceptance of Jesus.

This rejection has caused Christians of yore to resort to violence against Jews for centuries. In response, Jews have demonstrated a willingness to be tortured and killed rather than surrender their faith or forsake their Jewish identity.

But now, it's time to consider what Jews have to gain from accepting Jesus after all – not as the son of God but as a fallen son of our people, who fought to free the Jews from the cruel hand of the Romans. A man far more interested in the plight of Jews in this world than their salvation in the next.

CHAPTER 34

THIS WORLD AND THE NEXT

Christianity is extremely concerned with heaven and the afterlife. This urgency entails a list of things people can do to ensure that they receive the best rewards in the world to come. This is very different from Judaism, which focuses almost exclusively on proper behavior in this world.

The Hebrew Bible makes little mention of heaven or a celestial paradise. Judaism is more concerned with people's correct behavior in *this world* (which is the name of my organization that promotes universal Jewish values) than with their earning credit toward a comfortable place in heaven after death.

Jews do not follow Judaism for the purpose of reward in the afterlife. Indeed, a classical Jewish teaching from *Ethics of the Fathers* states, "Do not be one of those people who serves God in order to receive a reward."[305] We are to serve God for no other reason than that He is our creator and we must follow His dictates. Christian scholars I debate often ask, "Do you know where you're going?" My response to them is unequivocal. "My worship of God is not about me. It's not about saving myself from hell. I'm not here on this earth to spend my life accruing virtue so I get some divine reward. I don't worship God so it ultimately benefits me. I do it because I want to be in a relationship with Him. I do it because it's right. And I do it to make this world a better place. I love God unconditionally and unequivocally. Not because I expect anything in return."

Jews simply aren't that interested in the question of whether they're going to heaven or hell. The point of Judaism is to leave the world a better place than we found it. What happens next is of far lesser consequence. Jews focus on adhering to God's law in an effort to improve our lives and the lives of those around us.

The Jewish goal is to bring more light into the world, to help redeem it. To fight disease, end poverty, stop war, and push back bigotry and ignorance. Christians, of course, do the same but their emphasis is on using Jesus to seek salvation, both for themselves and others. While they care deeply about this world, their primary focus is on the next. Jews have no such motives for righteous action in this world.

The Christian emphasis on the afterlife is an acceptance of this life's futility. When missionaries urge people to accept Jesus and reach heaven, they convey a message that earthly life is filled with misery, and that only death gives life meaning. With faith in Jesus, Christians can avoid hell and reach heaven, redeeming their wretched earthly existence.

Jews have always rejected this message. Judaism is a religion of life. Moses tells the Jews, "See, I set before you today life and prosperity, death and destruction,"[306] and he urges the people, "Now, choose life."[307] Jews focus on enriching life in this world and have thus always rejected Christianity's emphasis on the next.

CHAPTER 35

DIVERSITY AND UNIFORMITY

According to Christian theology, there is but one truth. It is Jesus, and there can be no other way.

Judaism sees things differently. Neither rabbis nor Jewish sacred texts claim any exclusivity on truth. In no place does the Bible say those outside the Law of Moses are damned. On the contrary, Judaism has always recognized righteous gentiles, non-Jews who love God and are devoted to humanity. They will inherit the world to come along with the Jews.

According to the Talmud, "The rabbis taught: We support poor gentiles with the poor people of Israel, and we visit sick gentiles as well as the sick of Israel, and we bury the dead of the gentiles as well as the dead of Israel, because of the ways of peace."[308] Judaism is here to promote peace and harmony between nations rather than argue that we are saved while others are damned.

In the US we pride ourselves on tolerance for those unlike ourselves. We do our best to grin and bear the behavior of people we disagree with. Yet at a time when society appears utterly divided between right and left, rich and poor, pious and atheist, is this kind of tolerance really working for us, or is it driving us further apart?

I believe tolerance implies that we must take pains to suffer the presence of others, which is why I reject the term in favor of something else: mutual enrichment through difference. America is great specifically because of its leftward and rightward factions, which date back to the country's inception. Having different political parties is not something we tolerate but something we're proud of. Otherwise we'd be like China. Some of the best ideas that have come to conservatives have been generated by wishing to correct what they saw as liberal excess, and vice versa.

Rabbi Shneur Zalman of Liadi used the metaphor of a bird to convey the concept of mutual enrichment that comes through difference. A bird has two wings – on *opposite* sides of its body, without which it could not take flight. It requires antithetical propulsion in order to lift off. Had both wings been on the same side of its body, it would just flop over endlessly on its side.

I am a morally minded, passionately religious citizen of the United States, and I have fought hard for America to be a more Godly country. But I am well aware that countries with only religious priorities have descended into dangerous intolerance. Conversely, if America were comprised of strictly liberal and secular citizens, it could easily become a country without any permanent values. Having the two perspectives may create tension as they rub against each other, but it is healthy friction, so long as it is motivated by principal and conviction rather than hatred and fear.

Uniformity is always inferior to true multiculturalism. In communist, totalitarian societies, everyone has to be the same, or else. In North Korea, all citizens must submit to the whims of their "Dear Leader." In Stalin's Soviet Union, any deviation from the norm would draw suspicion and make it all the more likely that you would be made a non-person. Does Christianity really benefit from drawing from these examples and insisting that it alone has all truth?

Jews are required to treat gentiles with the same grace and kindness they treat one another. For instance, it is written, "One who sees a lost donkey of an idol worshipper must take care of it exactly the way he takes care of the lost donkey of an Israelite."[309] Elsewhere, the Talmud puts special responsibility on Jews, urging them to treat gentiles well, lest their bad behavior reflect badly on God. "It is more grievous to steal from a gentile because of the desecration of God's name."[310]

Judaism acknowledges that we live in a world of many religions, many creeds, and many paths to God – instead of consigning all the world's non-likeminded to perdition. Without mincing words, the Talmud states: "Righteous gentiles have a place in the world to come."[311] It is a compelling declaration by a religion that assures the inclusion into heaven of those who don't observe its tenants by virtue of their good deeds.

Elsewhere, the Talmud refers to a quote from the Book of Job: "'With justice and an abundance of kindness, He does not deal harshly' (Job 37:23) – God does not withhold reward from gentiles who perform His commandments."[312] Rabbi Yirmiyah is quoted as saying, "A gentile who fulfills His laws is like a [Jewish] high priest…a gentile who follows His commandments is [as righteous as the Jewish] high priest."[313] This is an incredible statement. Two thousand years ago, well before the advent of any kind of interfaith dialogue, when the Jews were being persecuted by the Romans and others for their faith, the Jews declared that a non-Jew who lives righteously is as holy as the Jewish high priest! As far as Judaism is concerned, diversity of opinion and creed are encouraged and expected not only in this world but in the next.

Christianity's insistence on resolute uniformity dates back to the Gospels themselves. In the Gospel of John, John the Baptist says, "Whoever believes in the Son has eternal life, but whoever rejects the Son will not see life, for God's wrath remains on him."[314] Later in the same Gospel, Jesus echoes this message of exclusivity and damnation of those outside the fold. "If you do not remain in me, you are like a branch that is thrown away and withers; such branches are picked up, thrown into the fire and burned."[315]

Jesus' alleged desire to have everyone conform to his standards appears elsewhere in the New Testament. For example, at the end of Mark, when Jesus comes back after the crucifixion, he tells the apostles, "Whoever believes and is baptized will be saved, but whoever does not believe will be condemned."[316] This is characteristic of Christian uniformity. But at the same time, it's impossible to imagine Jesus consigning his own people to damnation in this way – throwing into question whether this statement originated with him at all.

Nevertheless, inspired by such statements, Christianity has long maintained a unique claim on the truth. It is the only reality, and anyone who ignores or rejects it is living a lie that is destined to end in the soul's spiritual annihilation. Judaism rejects any emphasis on an exclusive spiritual truth. It is not a proselytizing religion, and Jews do not believe there is only one path to God.

The great monotheistic faiths have much to learn from one another. Christianity, Judaism, and Islam all derive from a common wellspring. All of us reach God in our own way. But in the pursuit of the higher goals, we can glean vital lessons from each other's strengths.

Every religion is known for certain characteristics: Christianity for its deep faith, Islam for its strong passion. Judaism stands alone not for its rejection of the divinity of Jesus or the prophecy of Mohammed, but for its singular concern with values, most of which are universal in nature. The values the Jewish people bequeathed the world are today no longer credited to the Jews. Jews gave the world the one true God. Today His name is Jesus or Allah. The Hebrew Bible's idea that all men are created equal today is called democracy. The Sabbath day is no longer Saturday but Sunday. The Ten Commandments have been subsumed under the rubric of secular humanism. But even if the Jews get little credit, there can be no doubt that these were universal Jewish contributions to humanity.

We all benefit from one another's contributions. The emphasis on spiritual exclusivity and one, unitary truth is precisely the spirit that has led to wars, crusades, pogroms, and ethnic cleansing, with each party claiming only they are right and consigning the existence of the other to "troublemaker" at best and "fit for extermination" at worst. Uniformity has never been a goal of Jewish thinkers.

Moses was the great lawgiver. Yet before that he labored as a shepherd. God was seeking the man that would deliver the Jews from Egypt. That person would have to be noble and command respect; charismatic and able to inspire the Jews to follow him; and wise, so he could mediate between the Jews and God. Moses was undoubtedly a paragon of all these virtues. But the Almighty selected him for a different reason.

According to the Midrash, one day Moses was minding the flock of his father-in-law. As he brought the sheep back from the pasture, he noticed one small sheep had been left behind. Moses left the flock for a moment to retrieve the straggler. At that instant God said, "This man shall be the leader of My people," and He revealed Himself in the form of the burning bush.[317]

Moses recognized that even a little sheep was an indispensable member of the community. Without it, the entire flock would be flawed and diminished. In the words of the Zohar, Moses was a *raayah mehemna*, a "trusted shepherd." He was so committed to the whole that he understood the value of every differing component part, big and small, fast and slow. Each constituent member or cog adds to the perfection of the whole. No member contribution is insignificant.

Judaism reveres this principle. The Almighty selected Moses because he was a leader who acknowledged that without the participation and contribution of every member, the nation would be deficient. Moses recognized the diversity inherent in creation, among people and animals, nations and ideas. This is how Judaism became the colorful and glorious community it is today.

The concept that more than one truth can exist simultaneously is one that Christianity has yet to fully embrace. Is the masculine truer than the feminine? Or do they complement each other? Is it not true that if the world were all masculine it would suffer from an excess of aggression and testosterone, untempered by the nurturing qualities of the feminine? And is it also not true that if the world were all feminine the linear qualities of the masculine would likewise be missing? The sexes need each other, are complemented by each other, and the joining together of the two brings new life. One is not more important or truer than the other. The orchestration of each component leads to a higher, more vibrant truth.

Christianity's insistence on exclusivity of truth runs counter to modern egalitarian thinking as well as ancient Jewish wisdom's acceptance of multiple paths to the one great truth, God. As stated in *Ethics of the Fathers*, "Do not scorn any man, and do not discount any thing. For there is no man who has not his hour, and no thing that has not its place."[318]

CHAPTER 36

EMBRACING JESUS AS A JEW

Jews have much to learn from Jesus – and from Christianity as a whole – without accepting Jesus' divinity. There are many reasons for accepting Jesus as a man of great wisdom, beautiful ethical teachings, and profound Jewish patriotism. Jews will gain much from re-embracing him as a hero.

For one thing, Jesus is one of the most famous Jews of all time. Yet he's been stolen from our community, stripped of his Jewishness, and in large measure made into an enemy of his people. For a Jew that loved his people to be transformed into the impetus for anti-Semitism is, to vastly understate the case, outrageous, offensive, and immoral. It is time to rebuild the bond between Jesus and his people and for Jews to reclaim one of their own.

I don't believe God gave only one truth. If you ask me whether I believe Judaism is true, my answer would be: of course it is. But unlike Christianity, which seeks for all to convert to its precepts, Judaism permits and encourages a diverse world. Judaism is not a proselytizing faith. While we believe Judaism is the true and right religion for us, we want Christians to observe Christianity, Muslims to celebrate Islam. Each should, in the words of my friend Marianne Williamson, honor their incarnation. For God, truth is like a puzzle. When you put all of the pieces together, the contributions from different faiths – under the umbrella of the Ten Commandments – build a higher truth.

There are crucial lessons that can only be found in the intersections between faiths. This is especially true with respect to Christians and Jews, given that Jesus was a Jew and Christianity derives from Judaism. The Jewish people have much to teach the Christians about community – about surviving in spite of overwhelming odds, and about standing up to implacable enemies. The Jews are a strong, undaunted, community-oriented people, and Christians could benefit a great deal from observing their example. But the Christians, likewise, have much to teach the Jewish people.

In my own experience, I count myself privileged to have been able to join my Christian Evangelical brethren on missions around the world. With them I've visited impoverished peoples in Africa, politically persecuted inhabitants of Zimbabwe, and families stricken by disaster in Haiti. From traveling and working with Christians I have learned a great deal – particularly from the passion for social justice so crucial to Christian activists today.

Both religious communities have their specialties – imagine how much stronger both would be if they learned openly from one another?

The ultimate reason Jews should pay careful heed to Jesus' Jewishness is both simple and compelling: the truth is important. A patriot of our people has been lost. Worse still, he's been painted as the father of a long and murderous tradition of anti-Semitism. This is a tragedy Jews can do something about. The time is now. By recognizing Jesus' Jewishness once it is free of its Christological wrapping, we can embrace once again a Jew who was martyred for defending our people.

PART V

RESTORING JUDEO-CHRISTIAN VALUES

CHAPTER 37

WHAT WE CAN ALL LEARN FROM JESUS

We've addressed the slanders and smears against Jews, outlined beliefs of Jesus that have been lost, and even detailed the timeless lessons that a Jewish Jesus has for Jews and Christians. But what is the value of it all in the end? Why should the religious status of an ancient martyr be of interest to us in our busy workaday lives? Does it really change anything for us to confront the essential Judaism of this deeply Christian figure? Do these tendentious theological debates amount to anything more than scholarly meandering, of little value to the real world?

To answer that question we should look to Christians the world over who are already rediscovering Jesus' Judaism. *Time Magazine* listed this concept in a cover story as one of their Top 10 Ideas Changing the World in 2008. "This is seismic," the editors exulted. "For centuries, the discipline of Christian 'Hebraics' consisted primarily of Christians cherry-picking Jewish texts to support the traditionally assumed contradiction between the Jews – whose alleged dry legalism contributed to their fumbling their ancient tribal covenant with God – and Jesus, who personally embodied God's new covenant of love. But today, seminaries across the Christian spectrum teach, as Vanderbilt University New Testament scholar Amy-Jill Levine says, that 'if you get the [Jewish] context wrong, you will certainly get Jesus wrong.'"[319]

What is it that people are rediscovering in the life of this ancient figure? I believe Christians are responding to an urgent need to humanize Jesus.

The problems that face us today are many: the financial crisis, the decline of our values, the deterioration of the family, rampant greed and materialism, the twin specters of terrorism and war. In order to reaffirm our innate sense of purpose in the face of hopelessness – to restore us when we are frightened – we must return to the values and principles that define us. The Jewish Jesus I have laid out before you embodies these Judeo-Christian values in truly inspiring ways. Restoring his Jewish identity makes available to us a flesh-and-blood hero who fought for what is right, in place of a celestial icon utterly detached from human experience. Christians can then take heart by looking to "Jesus the man" as a more accessible substitute for "Jesus the son of God."

This gets to the core of the principle difference between Judaism and Christianity. One is a value system based on struggle, and the other is based on perfection.

There are no perfect people in the Torah. Abraham makes mistakes in his handling of Ishmael. Isaac does the same with Esau. Jacob favors a child and creates jealousy among his children. King David sins with Bathsheba. Judaism is not premised on perfection. Do you know what the imperfect person has that the perfect person lacks? The ability to fight to do what is right. He struggles with his conscience. Goodness does not come naturally to him. He is challenged to behave selflessly and altruistically. He wrestles with his demons. When we fight for something, we demonstrate its worth.

Contrast this with other belief systems. Christianity is predicated on perfection, on the idea that Jesus was tempted but never fell. Unlike us, he had no predilection to evil. The same is true for Muslims and Mohammed. The mere suggestion that the prophet could sin could cause riots in today's streets. In Buddhism, the Buddha is the enlightened one, perfect. In the Hindu faith, Krishna is perfect. Even in the pantheon of great American heroes, our founding fathers were once portrayed as saints. I remember being taught as a young boy that George Washington never told a lie and that Abraham Lincoln walked miles to return a single penny. Both these stories were pure invention, but the idea was: How could you respect the founder of your nation if he was flawed?

But Judaism posits the opposite. Righteousness is found in struggle, rather than in perfection; and Judaism is full of men and women that wrestle with themselves, with big ideas, and with God Himself. The very word Israel means "he who wrestles with God." In this rich tradition, Jesus struggled against Rome, wrestling with oppression.

We need not fear a human Jesus. On the contrary, embracing his humanity allows Christians to identify with his struggle and emulate his commitment to righteousness.

Here in America, we also must wrestle with perfection. We are constantly being sold glossy images of people with perfect bodies, perfect résumés, perfect lifestyles. And convincing people of their inadequacy in relation to these paragons of physical, intellectual, moral, and aesthetic perfection is a thriving business.

But our truest heroes are those who are imperfect. Martin Luther King, Jr., universally regarded as a secular saint and a man I personally regard as perhaps the greatest American of the second half of the twentieth century, has been shown to have made mistakes. As revelations emerged that he struggled to hold his marriage together, Americans began to see him differently. His true greatness was thereby manifest: he was flawed and at times frail and still he accomplished a staggering amount, changing the course of our country as we knew it and restoring this great nation to its founding principles. You mean he was scared in front of those attack dogs and Bull Connor? He had to struggle to accomplish his goal of desegregation? He had to fight to do what's right? Now *that's* a great man.

Abraham Lincoln, the man who saved the union at its time of greatest strife, was far from perfect. Depressed, melancholy, he experienced periods of suicidal thoughts. The historian Joshua Shenk quotes Lincoln's dear friend Joshua Speed, who wrote, "Lincoln went Crazy...had to remove razors from his room – take away all Knives and other such dangerous things – &c – it was terrible."[320] Yet he triumphed over his brooding nature and became the very glue that ultimately sealed together a deeply divided nation.

The New Testament editors and Paul painted a divine figure of Jesus: What would he do if faced with our troubles? If Jesus is completely perfect and divine, we know very well what he would do: he would do the right thing. He's not human; he doesn't have to make difficult choices. He would do the right thing because he is not pulled to do otherwise. A Godly man would always choose righteousness.

And certainly, righteousness is an important ideal – we should all try to act justly. But what about the times when we feel drawn in a selfish, narcissistic direction? For inspiration, should we look to an angel or a real human hero shaded in with all the moral ambiguities that are part and parcel of being alive? To give Jesus the respect of seeing him as a man – a real man – humanizes the figure at the heart of Christianity and presents us with a model truly worth treasuring and emulating. What isn't nearly as helpful is a model of perfection we cannot achieve.

Those for whom life has been easy, those who never experience struggle, will never know the true taste of courage. They will never develop the ability to overcome obstacles, face the impossible, and do what is right. Untested, they will never firmly establish meaningful convictions.

The Zohar says that every time we choose to subdue and subjugate evil, God's glory rises higher. Every time we exert the effort to choose righteousness over selfishness, we show that righteousness is precious, and that God is a living presence we are prepared to fight for. Even when it is inconvenient. Even when it entails sacrifice. Even when we sometimes fall and are forced to pick ourselves up again. Struggle is where the infinite value of goodness is forged. That is why it's so important to engage in the struggle to elevate our life's values to a Godly station amid the gravitational pull in the opposite direction.

CHAPTER 38

JESUS AS A BRIDGE BETWEEN RELIGIONS

We live in an age where real rapprochement between religions is urgently necessary. I hardly need to point out we are today confronted by the interlinked crises of economic stagnation, political instability, and widespread violence. The West confronts the challenge of Radical Islam, both on the battlefield in Afghanistan and through terrorist attacks from afar. Jews and Christians have so much in common, we must unite behind our democratic values, defend the embattled State of Israel, and participate in a unified front against those who have vowed to defeat us.

Religious hatred and divisiveness plague the world. Leaders of Christianity and Judaism can ill afford trials of one-upmanship; we are not competitors, and religion is not a zero-sum game. Agreement between religions is not only valuable, but an outright necessity in our times.

Crucial to transforming the way Christianity and Judaism relate to one another is promulgating awareness of Jesus' heretofore ignored Jewishness. Naturally, I don't expect Christians to fully embrace my picture of Jesus and what he stood for, even as I bolster my arguments with pages from the New Testament. Mutual respect is crucial to the kind of rapprochement I'm advocating. Both Christians and Jews have much to learn from how devoted Jesus was to his people, from his belief in the sanctity of God's law, and the fact that the central figure in Christianity was one of the greatest Jewish patriots. We will find more commonalities with Jesus' Jewishness than we ever expected.

For one thing, Christian Evangelicals have proven themselves stalwart when it comes to foreign policy, fighting terrorists, and standing up to evil. They speak out and act against the genocide in Sudan, they are critical of President Obama's decision not to label as genocide the Turks' murder of the Armenians, and they have been fervent and moral opponents of Saddam Hussein, Hezbollah, and Hamas. Christian Evangelicals make up a huge proportion of our armed forces, and they have been leaders in our fight against Al-Qaeda and the Taliban in Afghanistan. They have been witnesses to the Taliban's horrific treatment of women, and their abuse and murder of innocent villagers for cooperating with NATO forces. Through this, their patriotism and devotion to democracy has only been heightened.

And yet, according to Paul and the Lucan editors, these beliefs appear to be in opposition to Jesus' own behavior. The Romans were a brutal occupying power, and he seems to readily submit to their torments. The Lucan editors would have us believe Jesus said, "Render unto Caesar what is Caesar's." Is that different from an Iraqi saying, Render unto Saddam Hussein what is Saddam's? Or an Iranian saying, Render unto Ahmadinejad what is his? How does this square with the modern Christian opposition to people who are no different than the Romans?

It is a revolutionary idea to balance the statements of Paul and the work of the Lucan editors with the Jewish truth about Jesus: he never voluntarily submitted, but rather fought the Romans with his last breath. We see this in the text of his own statements, when on the cross he lamented, "My God, my God, why have You forsaken me?"[321] Is this the statement of a humble, meek, and retiring man? Or is it a statement of defiance, a son of Israel living up to the definition of his name, "He who wrestles with God"? The Jesus who cried out to God to stop his suffering – the Jesus who demanded of God to render justice against the Romans and not abandon him, the innocent victim – is the same man who said, "I did not come to bring peace, but a sword."[322] He is a man ready to fight for what's right rather than live in humble resignation to a foreign, occupying power.

Jesus' last words on the cross, according to Matthew, demanding of God why he was forsaken, are echoed in the mouths of Jews today when we ask, "Where was God during the Holocaust?" God promised that goodness would triumph and the righteous would win out. So why was he being abandoned to the brutality of Rome on the cross? It was a travesty of justice, and Jews have forever inveighed even against God when it comes to seeming miscarriages of justice. "Will not the Judge of all the earth do right?"[323] is the challenge issued by Jesus' father Abraham against God when the Almighty threatens to destroy the inhabitants of Sodom and Gomorrah. How much more so when an innocent Jewish leader is being put to death by the wicked and evil Romans. In clamoring for salvation while on the cross, even if it appears to be an indictment of God's justice, Jesus is following in traditional Jewish footsteps. We forever defend innocent life and call God to account for His seeming abandonment of it.

One thing is clear. In crying out as he died, "My God, my God, why have You forsaken me?" Jesus is certainly not turning the other cheek.

If Evangelical Christians looked deeply and clearly at the Jewish Jesus outlined in this book, they would see a leader whose ideas agree with theirs more frequently than not. And rightly so. In my opinion, the depiction of Jesus as a figure who is passive in the face of evil is not something that resonates. If brutal occupiers are in our country, abusing human rights, we should fight them. Evangelical Christians in particular (who make up an estimated 60 percent of our armed forces) can embrace and draw strength from the redefinition of the hero that Judaism and Christianity hold in common.

CHAPTER 39

JESUS AND AMERICAN VALUES

Four premises form the foundation of Christian theology.

- First, people are born in sin and therefore will always fall short of righteousness. Man, left to his own devices, is damned.
- Second, because humans are in need of divine aid to be rescued from sin, God's son laid down his life to atone for human sin and rescue humanity from eternal damnation.
- Third, reposing faith in God's son, Jesus, makes his sacrifice effective for the individual believer.
- Fourth and finally, Jesus is the one and only road to salvation. Without Jesus we are condemned to hell, regardless of anything else we do.

It's striking how each of these ideas seems problematic in light of American values, yet Evangelical Christians are among the most patriotic citizens in our land.

Look at the first premise, which says people are born in sin. Fair enough, but the American justice system takes as its foundation the idea that a person's innocence should be presumed until guilt is proven in a court of law. Actions and evidence determine any verdict of innocence or guilt. The evenhanded fairness of American justice is a far cry from the Christian principle that man is born guilty and is innately sinful.

A second mismatch between Christianity's foundational premises and American values can be found in the idea of personal freedom.

Americans are a freedom-loving people, and the very nature of American liberty derives from the idea that people have been endowed with the right to self-determination. No one can hijack another's virtue, and no one can accept another's punishment for wrongdoing. With freedom, people own responsibility for their actions. Not so in Christian theology, which posits that Jesus, the sacrificial lamb, saves everyone from sin by absorbing his or her iniquity. The merit of his righteous deed grants everyone salvation. What about American independence and individualism, concepts that Christian Americans guard so zealously? This religious premise would seem to directly contradict them.

The third disagreement between American pragmatism and Christian theology occurs in everyday life. Over the course of a normal day, most Christians base their judgments on what a person does rather than what a person claims to believe. We all take seriously the old saw "Actions speak louder than words." After all, of what value is the intention to give 10 percent of your income to the poor unless you actually perform the act? Put another way, although a man may have lustful thoughts about a woman other than his wife, such thoughts surely cause less harm than actually committing adultery (Jimmy Carter's famous quote "I've committed adultery in my heart many times" notwithstanding). We would consider the man blameless so long as he remained faithful.

Not so according to Christian theology. Christian thinkers maintain that redemption and salvation are decided by belief rather than action. Protestant Christianity establishes that a person's good acts are insufficient for getting into heaven. Righteous faith rather than righteous action truly saves the person. Paul says it best: "That I may gain Christ and be found in him, not having a righteousness of my own that comes from the law, but that which is through faith in Christ – the righteousness that comes from God and is by faith."[324]

What would Jesus really have thought of this doctrine? He was, after all, an observant Jew, who kept all the mitzvahs and all the commandments of the Torah. So scrupulously did he observe the law that he famously said, in the Book of Matthew, "For truly I tell you, until heaven and earth disappear, not the smallest letter, not the least stroke of a pen, will by any means disappear from the Law until everything is accomplished. Therefore anyone who sets aside one of the least of these commands and teaches others accordingly will be called least in the kingdom of heaven, but whoever practices and teaches these commands will be called great in the kingdom of heaven."[325] In incontrovertible opposition to the claims in the previous paragraph, this declares unmistakably that righteous acts save the individual, not "correct" belief or professions of faith.

Jesus' declaration accords far more with American sensibilities than Christian doctrine. In the United States, we judge people by their actions, not by what they believe. The Pilgrims came to America in the seventeenth century precisely to escape persecution for their "wrong" beliefs. American democracy is about doing, saying, and voting for what we believe in, transforming those beliefs into action. Jesus, too, preached moral empowerment to draw closer to God, and the need for individual repentance rather than collective dependency on one individual sacrifice.

Finally, there is the bedrock belief that acceptance of Jesus is the only way to get to heaven – and all who fail to are damned. This idea that we should live our lives *in order to get into heaven* runs counter to basic American values, as well. John Kennedy expressed it best. "Ask not what your country can do for you; ask what you can do for your country." You're not supposed to do the right thing for a reward. Rather, the action is valuable in and of itself. But for some Christians, belief in Jesus becomes the royal road to salvation, a means rather than an end.

In this country we revere those who live justly and patriotically with little or no reward. Our military men and women offer a prime example. Wall Street bankers, by contrast, are far less respected. Much of what they do is perceived as geared toward personal profit. Yet in Christianity, we have an entire theological construct that would seem to emphasize the "payoff" over the good behavior itself.

If Jesus is the sole key to salvation, what is the fate of the Jews? Jesus, a deeply religious Jew, who fought for his people's independence from Rome, would never agree with a belief that consigns his own people to eternal damnation. Such an idea aligns neither with American values nor with the heroic Jesus that actually lived and died for his people.

This is not to say Christian doctrine is wrong. But it may prompt a Christian who studies the Jewishness of Jesus to say to him- or herself, "Okay – I believe in the primacy of faith over works. That's part of the essence of my religion. However, now that I see the way Jesus actually approached this issue, I am expanding my view of the matter. I accept the possibility that faith can be expressed through deeds. After all, the faithfulness and goodness of non-Christians make them all the more precious to God. Perhaps this was the lesson Jesus intended me to take from his example after all."

Christianity and Judaism remain separate faiths. But by finding their common ground through a discovery of the Jewish Jesus, we strengthen America's Judeo-Christian values. And that is, in the end, the essence of what I seek to accomplish.

CHAPTER 40

THE HYPHEN THAT UNITES US

Religious people are now grappling with an alarming state of affairs: Americans are losing faith in the relevance of Judeo-Christian values.

Judaism is in danger. Fifty percent of Jewish young people choose to marry outside the faith, assimilating and putting the future survival of our nation in doubt. Israel is being delegitimized by hateful enemies the world over and is besieged by enraged enemies. Jews would do well to capitalize on Christian overtures of goodwill so as to remain strong in the face of adversity.

Christianity, too, seems to be on the ropes in many parts of the world, particularly in Europe. But even in the United States, there are serious challenges to Christian faith. American Christians are a good and Godly people – of this I have no doubt. However, the religion's moral authority has diminished in recent years. Over time, Christianity has lost some of its heart, emphasizing an austere morality that narrowly defines religious ethics and family values as opposition to homosexuality and abortion. The narrowness of the American Christian approach to values and its near obsession with these twin issues – especially gay marriage – is allowing for moral decay to set in in America, seeing as it highlights these peripheral issues to the exclusion of nearly everything else. The noble goals of Christianity are undermined every time Christian thinkers, politicians, and public figures sound in any way bigoted or come across as hypocritical.

The powerful Christian community in America finds itself at a crossroads. The eighty million born-again Christians who had such a pronounced role in President George W. Bush's two electoral victories lost their political muscle in the 2008 presidential election. Bill Maher and a host of other opponents of organized religion have made a financial killing by portraying religious people as self-satisfied oafs who swallow faith uncritically and send their money to charlatan televangelists flying around in gas-guzzling G5s.

What were the buzzwords of the 2010 election? Spending, deficits, and earmarks – all worthy subjects of discussion, but what happened to values? The sad truth is that Evangelical Christians have become politically marginalized by clinging to homosexuality as their bogeyman. Rather than focusing on the divorce rate, the sexualization of younger and younger teens, or the ongoing collapse of the American family, it seems Evangelical Christian pundits and politicians would prefer to have us talking about banning gays from serving in the military, and obsessing over their right to marriage and adoption. Are Evangelical Christians really ready to lay all of our society's ills at the feet of gays?

America has serious social problems. Fifty percent of all marriages end in divorce. Forty million American marriages are platonic. One out of three American women is on antidepressants. Innumerable American men are addicted to pornography. Our teenagers have unacceptably high rates of pregnancy and alcoholism. However, I cannot name a single initiative that appeared on a ballot to combat any of these problems, save for Proposition 8 in California that sought to ban gay marriage. Let me ask my Evangelical brothers and sisters: Do gays pose the biggest challenge to the sanctity of heterosexual marriage? Or do straight people and the 50 percent divorce rate constitute a much more significant threat?

During the Obama/McCain presidential campaign, I tried hard to make the possible tax-deductibility of marital counseling a campaign issue. Studies show that when couples get proper counseling, the vast majority of these troubled marriages survive. If counseling were declared tax-deductible, couples would have access to the crucial support they may otherwise find unaffordable. But it's nigh impossible to talk seriously about the real causes of marital breakdown, or their solutions, due to the ongoing gay marriage obsession.

The argument that stopping gay marriage is the key to saving the institution of marriage in general, and the American family in particular, is spurious. Would anyone seriously suggest that if there were no gays in America there would no longer be a 50 percent heterosexual divorce rate? Are we really looking to scapegoat gays for the fact that sraight people can't seem to remain in love and married? Truth be told, we heterosexuals need no assistance from gays in destroying the institution of marriage, having done a fine job of it ourselves, thank you very much. Indeed, the only men who seem to still want to marry in America are gay! They're the ones who are petitioning the United States Supreme Court for the right to marry, while straight men break out in a rash whenever their girlfriends bring up the word *marriage.*

The opponents of gay marriage have been saying that their opposition is all about protecting the family and the institution of marriage. But gays marrying has nothing to do with heterosexuals divorcing, and the real crisis in the American marriage is not that people of the same sex want to get hitched but that people of the opposite sex don't want to stay together.

My parents divorced when I was eight. There were no gays around to blame. It was mid-1970s America, and gays scarcely came out of the closet, let alone married. The very thought was inconceivable. My parents did not argue because they saw two gay women holding hands at an airport. They did not bicker because a rainbow flag hung outside a bar in our neighborhood. They did not decide to end their marriage because they could not agree on how the institution of marriage should be defined. Rather, their marriage ended because it ran out of love.

Their split scarred me for life, just as it does many other children of divorce, as a famous study published in the *American Sociological Review* demonstrates.[326] The study found little to no impact on children prior to divorce but significant decreases in performance in math and social skills at the time of and following the divorce, which gives the lie to the belief that children are worse off seeing parents fight than seeing them divorce. And no, I do not believe that parents should stay together for the sake of their children. Children should not be jailers. But less so do I believe we should fool ourselves about the effects of divorce on children.

My parents love me and did not want me to suffer. But they could not, or chose not to, get along. I have since devoted much of my life to keeping families together and regularly counsel marriages in crisis. In the twenty-two years I have done so, no straight couple has ever told me that their problems stem from gays wanting to marry. In most cases their marital unhappiness resulted from falling out of love or losing attraction, or one of the partners had been unfaithful. Money problems may have eaten away at the fabric of the relationship. Parents or other family members might have intervened and caused friction. Or the pressures of life made it impossible for the couple to spend quality time together. But none of the problems I have counseled could be traced back to gay marriage.

The truth is that the thirty-year fight over gay marriage, largely conducted by our Evangelical brothers, has been a massive distraction for America that has prevented us from focusing on skyrocketing divorce, the growing culture of male womanizing, women feeling unreasonably old, fat, and unattractive, the fixation of husbands and wives on celebrity relationships that deprives their own marriages of oxygen, and the dumbing down of America through moronic reality TV. My God, we can't even talk about runaway materialism in our culture.

For some, Christianity seems to flourish by identifying godless enemies. God battles Lucifer. Jesus vies against the anti-Christ. Red-state Christians contend with hedonistic blue-state liberals, the godless barbarians at the gate. The forces of light always fight with the forces of darkness. It is a vision that has inspired many over the years, but in the process, Christians have inadvertently made Jesus – and by extension Christianity itself – very divisive.

To salve this contentious, embattled worldview, Christians would do well to pay renewed attention to Jesus, his humanity, and the values he held dear. Embracing his proven Jewish characteristics, allying with a willing Jewish community, and adopting his passionate patriotism, respect for tradition, and vision of a redeemed world could prove to be American Christianity's best hope.

The Christian worldview must return to the Judeo-Christian values on which our civilization was founded. *Judeo-Christian* is a strange word – a hyphenated term that unites two very different religions and ways of looking at the world.

Hyphens, though unassuming, can be frightening things. They draw together unrelated concepts to bring new, unforeseen chimeras into the world. Americans have only gradually come to terms with hyphenated Americans: African-Americans, Jewish-Americans, Muslim-Americans. A hundred years ago Woodrow Wilson typified this line of thinking by saying "Any man who carries a hyphen about with him carries a dagger that he is ready to plunge into the vitals of this Republic whenever he gets ready."

Of course we are all Americans, equal and unhyphenated. And the hyphen between Judaism and Christianity is no dagger and doesn't have to be a barrier either. It is a bridge that spans a divide – a divide that, admittedly, has been widened by millennia of mutual distrust and rampant anti-Semitism. But for the first time in history, that divide is growing smaller.

If I can leave my readers with one ringing message after the mountain of scriptural and historical information you've read in this book, it is this: The hyphen between Jewish and Christian values is Jesus himself. Both religions share him, looking to him from opposite sides of a chasm. He can bring us closer to one another, if only we are brave enough to allow for understanding him in a new light.

At a time when the world flails in search of values, strangled by materialism, divisiveness, instability, doubt, and unrest, we must return to the basic ideals we share in common. All of these are to be found in the life and lessons of Jesus of Nazareth, lover of Israel, rebel against Rome, Jewish hero, and the inspiration for innumerable acts of Christian charity.

In our hyphenated world, the Jewish Jesus has the power to bring disparate peoples together. Our civilization will be all the stronger if Jews and Christians alike accept Jesus for who he really was: a driving force for liberty, democracy, and Jewish identity in a world ruled by the tyranny and brutality of Rome. In his time, as in our time – as in Judeo-Christian civilization in years to come – the fight for redemption and independence continues.

Now, Jews and Christians can answer the clarion call for liberty and a renewal of values together, even as we remain distinct and separate faiths. We can, for the first time, set the stage for Jews and Christians to come together to achieve Godly goals and virtuous ends through the personality of Jesus himself, even as we both understand him in completely different ways.

JEWISH SOURCES ON THE DEATH OF JESUS

Throughout this book, I've endeavored to address all arguments opposing the true Jewish nature of Jesus, and in so doing, to emphasize his identity as a political rather than a religious rebel. I have made my argument largely from the pages of the New Testament, thereby demonstrating that from Christian scripture itself we can glean the truest nature of the Jewishness of Jesus and how he has been misrepresented throughout the ages. Yet there is still an important detail that remains to be addressed: the Jewish sources, and what they have to say specifically about the death of Jesus.

On countless occasions, numerous Christian-scholar debating partners have cited both the Talmud and the Jewish sage Maimonides in an attempt to prove the Jews killed Jesus. Based on the lines they cite, it would indeed appear their assertions are correct. But if we look at these texts in context, the reality revealed is very different. The Jesus whom the Talmud and Maimonides discuss *cannot* be the same rabbi and Jewish patriot written about in this book, and whom Paul cites as the founder of Christianity. In short, the Yeshu whose death is discussed in the Talmud is not Jesus of Nazareth.

My opponents often cite the Talmudic passage below, which seems to state that the Jewish high court had condemned Jesus, or "Yeshu," to death.

> It is taught: On the eve of Passover they hung Yeshu and the crier went forth for forty days beforehand declaring that

"[Yeshu] is going to be stoned for practicing witchcraft, for enticing and leading Israel astray. Anyone who knows something to clear him should come forth and exonerate him." But no one had anything exonerating for him and they hung him on the eve of Passover. Ulla said: Would one think that we should look for exonerating evidence for him? He was an enticer, and God said, "Show him no pity or compassion, and do not shield him" (Deuteronomy 13:9). Yeshu was different because he was close to the government.[327]

What is actually happening here? Someone named Yeshu is executed on the eve of Passover. As was done before any execution, the court searched for witnesses who could clear his name. Ulla questioned this practice, for an enticer, due to a biblical mandate, was not afforded such consideration. The Talmud answers that Yeshu was different. Because of his government connections, the court tried to search for any reason not to execute him so as to avoid upsetting the authorities.

No doubt, there are some similarities to the story of Jesus. Simultaneously, there are equally obvious differences. In the end, disagreements between Jesus' and Yeshu's stories force us to conclude that Jesus is not identical to the Yeshu identified in the passage.

In the first place, the timing does not match up. In the Synoptic Gospels, Jesus is executed on Passover itself, not the eve of Passover. This is highly significant. If Jesus did not die on the first night of Passover, the very idea of the Eucharist would be invalidated. The tradition of the Eucharist is founded on the idea that Jesus ate the Passover seder's matzo – a wafer-like bread – and wine. If he instead died before the seder, this practice would not have arisen. Furthermore, the Talmudic claim that Yeshu was executed on the day before Passover must be accurate, for, as explained earlier, the Sanhedrin never put anyone to death on a Jewish holiday. Doing so was prohibited by Jewish law.

Just as the timing fails to align, the cast of characters differs between the two stories. The Yeshu cited in the Talmud was executed by a Jewish court, not by the Romans as the Gospels relate. In the time that Yeshu lived, the Jewish courts had the power to enforce capital punishment, yet they were cautious because the courts were ruled by the Pharisees while the king was a Sadducee. This was not the case during the Roman occupation, when Jesus lived. And certainly, there is no indication in the New Testament that Jesus had any friends in the government. On the contrary, Jesus was a committed thorn in the side of the Roman authorities.

In the Talmudic narrative, a number of students are put to death along with Yeshu. These were his "five disciples, Matthai, Nakai, Nezer, Buni, and Todah."[328] With the sole exception of Matthai, or Matthew, which was (and remains) a common name, the students' names are completely other than those of Jesus' apostles. In contrast, the New Testament says two criminals were crucified along with Jesus, and certainly none of his disciples.

The chronology is off as well, by no less than a century. The name Jesus, or Yeshu in Hebrew, was very common in the Talmudic period. The Jewish historian Josephus lists about twenty major Jesus-Yeshu figures in his histories.[329] A good example is the farmer Jesus, the son of Ananias, who while standing in the Temple suddenly began to cry out: "A voice against Jerusalem and the holy house.... A voice against the whole people."[330] This Jesus went through the streets of Jerusalem day and night, crying out: "Woe, woe to Jerusalem!" He predicted the destruction of the Second Temple before it happened.

As similar as he may seem, this cannot be Christianity's Jesus. Josephus says this Jesus began his predictions of the Temple's destruction just six years before it happened in 70 CE. He was alive to watch as the Romans sacked Jerusalem. By this time, the Jesus of the New Testament had been dead for almost forty years.

So who was the Talmud's Yeshu? The Talmud identifies him as a student of Yehoshua ben Perachyah, a sage who died at least one hundred years before the Jesus of the New Testament was born. The Talmud tells the story of how this Yeshu of Nazareth, later to be executed, began as a rebellious student of Rabbi Yehoshua:

> R. Yehoshua ben Perachyah…came to a certain inn. His hosts stood up for him in a display of great honor, and they continued to accord him much honor. He sat and was praising his hostess: "How nice is this hostess," meaning, "how pleasing are her deeds." Mistaking his teacher's intent, one of his students [Yeshu] said to him: "Rabbi, she is not beautiful, for her eyes are round!" [R. Yehoshuah ben Perachyah] said to [this student]: "Wicked one! In matters such as these you occupy yourself?!" He took out four hundred horns, and excommunicated [the student]. Every day, [the student] would come before [R. Yehoshua ben Perachyah] to beg forgiveness, and [R. Yehoshua ben Perachyah] would not receive him, i.e., he refused to forgive him. One day, when [R. Yehoshua ben Perachyah] was reciting *Krias Shema* [the prayer declaring the unity of God during which talking is forbidden], [the student] came before him yet again. This time, [R. Yehoshua ben Perachyah] had intended to accept him, and pardon him. Being unable to talk at the moment, he motioned to [the student] with his hand that he would receive him as soon as he finished reciting *Krias Shema*. But [the student] thought that he was pushing him away yet again, and despaired of ever attaining his teacher's forgiveness. So he went and stood a brick on end, and worshiped it as an idol. Subsequently [R. Yehoshua ben Perachyah] said to him: "Repent!" But [this student] replied to him: Thus have I received a tradition from you: Whoever sins and causes others to sin

is not given the opportunity to repent. As the Master said: [This student] practiced sorcery, and incited others and led them astray, and caused Israel to sin.[331]

The Talmud explains that this Jesus left the monotheistic path of Judaism and began serving idols. Yehoshua ben Perachyah died about one hundred and thirty years before the destruction of the Temple, which makes it impossible for Christianity's Jesus to have been his disciple. Clearly, then, the Yeshu discussed in the Talmud is not the same Yeshu whom history remembers as the founder of Christianity.

Nevertheless, some historians insist the Yeshu in the Talmud is Jesus. Their proof? In one manuscript of the Talmud he is called Yeshu the Notzri, which could mean Jesus the Nazarene. However, only one of the approximately four distinct manuscripts of the Talmud available uses the title Notzri. None of the other manuscripts contain that title, which means it could be a later interpolation, as medieval commentators suggest.[332]

Not only that, but the word Notzri does not even necessarily mean Nazarene. While centuries later it was used to refer to Christians, in the form of *Notzrim* or *Netzarim,* it could also have been a term used to refer to many strong communities. The name "Ben Netzar" was used in the Talmud to refer to the famous chief of robbers Odenathus of Palmyra.[333]

Between timing, chronology, and content, there is no way to align the Yeshu of the Talmud with Jesus of Nazareth, without interpreting far beyond the bounds of what the text allows.

MAIMONIDES

The other citation I frequently confront in debates is from Maimonides, the great Jewish philosopher. He, too, bases his discussion of the death of Jesus on the previously quoted text from the Talmudic tractate Sanhedrin describing how Yeshu was executed on the eve of Passover. And, whoever Maimonides was talking about, it likewise cannot be the Jesus of the New Testament.

Maimonides writes: "Jesus of Nazareth...impelled people to believe that he was a prophet sent by God to clarify perplexities in the Torah, and that he was the Messiah that was predicted by each and every seer. He interpreted the Torah and its precepts in such a fashion as to lead to their total annulment, to the abolition of all its commandments, and to the violation of its prohibitions. The sages, of blessed memory, having become aware of his plans before his reputation spread among our people, meted out fitting punishment to him."[334]

We cannot take this at face value. While this and a few other Jewish sources seem to indicate the Jews killed Jesus, all were written at the very least many hundreds of years after the events in question. They cite no convincing evidence, and sure enough, are based on legend rather than fact. Many of them seem to have been written out of a Jewish sense of bravado. As a way of striking back at their aggressors and empowering a weak, emasculated Jewish nation, some Jewish writers took comfort in writing they were not being persecuted for nothing and had actually killed the Christian god.

One of the most famous of these works is a book called *Toldos Yeshu ha-Notzri*, which includes fantastical stories about Jesus and the rabbis. One such tale involves Jesus reading the name of God inside the Temple, writing it down on a piece of paper, cutting his skin, and hiding the paper in the wound so the Temple guards could not see it. Once outside, Jesus removed the paper, read the name aloud, and began to fly around the Temple. Seeing this, the Jewish religious authorities read the name of God, flew above Jesus, and urinated on him so as to desecrate the name and end his magic.

This story is clearly not factual and was written many centuries after Jesus' death. The *Toldos Yeshu ha-Notzri* collection of stories was written in a time of oppressive anti-Semitism. It was intended to instill pride in the children and adults who were abused by Christian powers at the time. It had nothing to do with the historical truth of Jesus, and makes little sense to us today, pulled from its original context.

Neither from the Talmud, nor from any other Jewish source, is there any legitimate evidence to suggest the Jews killed Jesus. Every story relates to another Yeshu, or Jesus, a name very common in Temple times and a period rife with people claiming to be the messiah. All other sources are fictitious. There remains no proof, either Christian or Jewish, of any genuine animosity between Jesus and the religious authorities of his day; to the contrary, the New Testament says explicitly that the rabbis saved the life of Jesus when it was threatened by Herod. Had the rabbis wanted Jesus dead, they could have finished him off right then and there when the brutal king sought his scalp.

ACKNOWLEDGMENTS

This book has been a project of many years, taking longer to write than any of my previous books. It has benefited from many steady hands and editors who have assisted me in presenting the complex material in the most accessible light possible.

Principal among them are Brandon Proia, who prior to this assignment had no extensive exposure to biblical scholarship, but who was an absolute trooper in taking my original manuscript and shifting the order to make it more readable and allow the argument to flow more naturally. Having finished this work, Brandon is now the most religious man that ever lived and, though not Jewish, can be seen walking the streets of Manhattan with a long bushy beard and side-curls, slaughtering goats.

Monica Klein also went through the entire manuscript, simplifying the language and attempting to shorten it by fifty thousand words by simply removing the word "I." I explained to her that you can't tamper with a masterpiece, and what she was doing was akin to taking a jackhammer to the *Mona Lisa*. Still she carried on and the result was a much more readable book, although, truth be told, I intentionally made the manuscript somewhat imperfect from the outset in order to endow her life with meaning and purpose. No need to thank me, Monica. It's just part of my giving nature.

Other hands who dared defile my original writing include my dear friend Yehuda Efune, who, schooled in the King's English, did extensive research to help support my arguments; and Ben Kiel and Jon Myerov, who assisted in piecing together my first twenty-odd drafts into something resembling legibility.

My debating partner Dr. Michael Brown, a Jew who converted to Christianity and is now a Christian scholar and missionary who runs a renowned missionary school where I was even invited to speak about – believe it or not – *not* proselytizing Jews, has become a dear friend through our exchanges, although, were you to watch our debates on YouTube you would scarcely believe it. Our take-no-prisoners approach to debates, in which we publicly savage each other, is usually followed by warm dinners of him eating succulent foods and me eating moldy, King-David-era bread, which is usually about the only kosher thing I can find in the cities in the South where we debate. Still, our exchanges have served as one of the sources of inspiration for this book. I love Mike – he's an amazing guy, especially when he's not trying to get Jews to believe in the divinity of Jesus. But it's time Mike came back to his people and to the religion that Jesus actually practiced, which is the one Mike was born into, Judaism. No doubt, when Mike reads the overwhelmingly compelling arguments in my book he will be knocked out by the incontrovertible logic and decide to have his bar mitzvah again. Just remember, Mike, this time the checks come to me.

Ilan Greenfield of Gefen Publishing House is an amazing man and a skilled and professional publisher, as well as a gentleman through and through. We were able to hammer out a contract verbally from almost the first time we met that was then signed with great alacrity, before he realized that the title to his company had now reverted to me. Don't worry, Ilan, I plan to do great things with Gefen, beginning with an *Encyclopedia of Shmuley's Childhood and Upbringing*, available at fine bookstores everywhere, and of course as an e-book on Amazon. It is an honor to have this book published in Israel and distributed worldwide, a beautiful metaphor for the light that the Jewish people are meant to disseminate throughout the world, with Israel as its base. And what better light than a book bearing my name. (Ed. – That's enough talking about yourself, Shmuley. Now move on.) (Shmuley – No, it's not. I've barely even begun.)

The deep and inspiring faith of my Christian brothers and sisters, especially Evangelicals, is another source of inspiration behind this book. When I lived in Oxford, England, and started my student organization that would later number in the thousands, I was amazed at the untold number of Christian students who not only wanted to be part of our organization, but came several nights a week to volunteer to work doing the mailing lists, setting up for our big Sabbath dinners, putting up large portraits of me throughout the university, and generally keeping our operation going. This was great because it gave me more time to play solitaire. But it also sent me on a journey to more deeply explore Christianity and its capacity to inspire goodness and love of Israel and the Jewish people in its adherents. Evangelicals' love of Israel, as well as Catholic admiration and respect for Judaism, is as responsible for this book as anything else, and I am especially grateful for the warm reception accorded to me by Pope Benedict XVI when I visited with him via my friend Gary Krupp in May of 2010 (yes, that actually did happen). I was honored to accommodate the pope's request to have an autographed copy of my picture.

In every book I thank my parents and siblings for their love and support. My mother and father taught me love of God and love of God's children. Thank you, Abba and Mommy, for all you taught me through your living example. And thank you for giving the world such a beautiful gift in the form of me.

To my siblings, Sarala, Bar Kochva, Ateret, and Chaim Moishe, I thank you for nurturing that gift with loving wedgies and beating me to a pulp as a kid so I could understand that being a Jew really does involve constant suffering. You are the greatest siblings in the world and I love you.

My kids are the light of my life, and the source of most of my debt. It's difficult writing any book when you have nine kids nagging you through most of the day – and all of the night. Which just proves that this book is a true miracle. Thank you, Mushki, Chana, Shterny, Mendy, Shaina, Yosef, Dovid Chaim, and little baby Cheftziba (I know, I know, you're not a baby anymore, you're a big girl, right?). I also, for the first time, want to thank the man who should be my son-in-law by the time this book is published. Thank you, Arik, for marrying Mushki. No doubt marrying the daughter of a rabbi who has just written a book on the kosher Jesus has filled you and your entire family with great pride. Welcome to the family.

To my wife, the luckiest woman in the whole world, what can I say other than you won the lottery. My wife, Debbie, is the living personification of the pure heart religion can foster in a human being. She is my superior in all things; there is nothing I do that is not blessed by her being at my side. That is, so long as I make money, the failure of which she has made clear might preclude her from continuing to be at my side. So God bless you all for buying this book. May you buy the other twenty-five I've written, some of which have sold about twenty-five copies.

Finally, and most importantly, to God Almighty, Master of heaven and earth, He Who fills the infinite expanse of space and is the source of all blessing and life, thank you, Lord, for loving me, nurturing me, guiding me, and preserving me. I could do nothing without you, Lord. I only hope and wish that my life's efforts accrue to Your glory.

May the righteous and true Messiah of Israel arrive soon and usher in an era of eternal peace, blessing, and kinship among all of God's children. And while I do not believe it is Jesus, I look forward to sharing a more perfect world with my Christian brothers and sisters in a world suffused with love and joy.

Rabbi Shmuley Boteach
Autumn 2011
Englewood, NJ

NOTES AND SOURCES

1. Krister Stendahl, *Paul among Jews and Gentiles, and Other Essays* (Philadelphia: Fortress Press, 1976), 4.

2. Jerry Falwell, *Listen America* (New York: Doubleday, 1980), 107, 112.

3. Hyam Maccoby, *Revolution in Judaea: Jesus and the Jewish Resistance* (New York: Taplinger, 1980).

4. Ibid., 48–49.

5. Josephus, *Wars of the Jews*, book VII.

6. See, for example, Martin Luther, *On the Jews and Their Lies* (Reedy, WV: Liberty Bell Publications, 2004).

7. Matthew 3:7 NIV.

8. Ibid. 16:5–12 NIV.

9. Numbers 25:13 NIV.

10. 2 Kings 2:11 NIV.

11. Readers interested in an even deeper examination of the rabbinic sources of Jesus' teachings should look to Rabbi Moshe Reiss's *Christianity: A Jewish Perspective*, which compiles all of the available textual evidence to prove Jesus' Jewish intellectual heritage. Its full text can be found online at http://moshereiss.org/christianity.html.

12. Matthew 6:24 NIV; Luke 16:13 NIV.

13. Deuteronomy 6:5 NIV.

14. Matthew 5:5 NIV.

15. Psalms 37:11 NIV.

16. Matthew 7:7 NIV.

17. Jeremiah 29:13 NIV.

18. Matthew 7:5 NIV.

19. Arachin 16b.

20. Shabbat 31a.

21. Darrell J. Fasching, *The Jewish People in Christian Preaching* (Lewiston, NY: Edwin Mellen Press, 1985), 67.

22. Leviticus 19:18 NIV.

23. Matthew 7:12 NIV.

24. Mark 12:31 NIV.

25. Exodus 23:4 NIV.

26. Matthew 5:43 NIV.

27. Ibid. 6:15 NIV.
28. Rosh Hashanah 17a.
29. For a detailed exploration of the rabbinic precedents for Jesus' parables and allegories, see Craig L. Blomberg, *Interpreting the Parable* (Downers Grove, IL: InterVarsity Press, 1990), 29–60.
30. In this chapter I have relied on the findings of David Biven, whose study of Jesus' borrowings from rabbinical modes of reasoning provides conclusive proof of Jesus' intellectual heritage. For further reading, see David Biven, "Principles of Rabbinic Interpretation: Kal Va-Homer," Jerusalem Perspective Online, http://www.jerusalemperspective.com/Default.aspx?tabid=27a ndArticleID=1495.
31. Codified by Rabbi Hillel, the seven laws include *gezerah shavah* (similar laws, similar verdicts), *kelal u-ferat* and *ferat u-kelal* (general and particular, particular and general), and four other methods of seeking understanding based on examining the content and context of various passages.
32. Tosefta Pesachim 9:2.
33. Sanhedrin 6:5.
34. Luke 12:24 NIV.
35. Matthew 7:11 NIV.
36. Luke 12:27–28 NIV.
37. Mark 2:23 NIV.
38. Ibid. 2:24 NIV.
39. Ibid. 2:25–26 NIV.
40. 1 Samuel 21 NIV.
41. Mark 2:27 NIV.
42. Yoma 85b.
43. Ibid.
44. John 7:23 NIV.
45. Matthew 15:10–14 NIV.
46. Ibid. 15:11 NIV.
47. Midrash Psalms 2.
48. Matthew 15:1–3 NIV.
49. Josephus, *Jewish Antiquities* (London: Wordsworth, 2003), 581.
50. See Morton Smith, *Jesus the Magician: Charlatan or Son of God?* (New York: Harper and Row, 1978), 215.
51. John 2:1–11 NIV.
52. 2 Kings 4:42–44 NIV.
53. Mark 6:41–45 NIV; Matthew 14:19–21, 15:36–38 NIV; Luke 9:16–17 NIV; John 6:1–14 NIV.

54. Matthew 14:15–21 NIV.
55. Ibid. 15:32–38 NIV.
56. Smith, *Jesus the Magician*, 156–57.
57. Mark 4:37–41 NIV.
58. Psalms 107:25–30 NIV.
59. Jonah 1 NIV; also see Randel Helms, *Gospel Fictions* (Amherst, NY: Prometheus Books, 1988), 76–78.
60. Mark 6:47–52 NIV.
61. Matthew 14:28–33 NIV.
62. Luke 11:20 NIV.
63. Pesachim 112b.
64. Kiddushin 29b.
65. Isaiah 35:5 NIV.
66. Luke 10:23–24 NIV.
67. Megillah 7a.
68. 2 Kings 4:32–37 NIV.
69. Mark 8:12 NIV.
70. John 4:48 NIV.
71. Mark 5:43, 7:36 NIV.
72. Ibid. 9:20 NIV.
73. Josephus, *Jewish Antiquities*, 323.
74. Tales of the Patriarchs, 1QapGen 21.28–29.
75. For a deeper examination of the source for this citation, see Meir Bar-Ilan, *Exorcism by Rabbis, Talmud Sages, and Their Magic*, http://faculty.biu.ac.il/~barilm/exorcism.html.
76. Luke 7:12–15 NIV.
77. Mark 5:38–42 NIV.
78. John 11:43–44 NIV.
79. 1 Kings 17:19–23 NIV.
80. Deuteronomy 28:1–12 NIV.
81. Hyam Maccoby, *The Mythmaker: Paul and the Invention of Christianity* (New York: Barnes and Noble, 1986), 185.
82. Matthew 8:10 NIV.
83. Luke 7:4–5 NIV.
84. John 19:4–6 NIV.
85. Mark 15:39 NIV.
86. Luke 23:2 NIV.
87. Michael L. Brown, *Our Hands Are Stained with Blood* (Shippensburg, PA: Destiny Image Publishers, 1992), xv.

88. Quoted in Georges Friedmann, *The End of the Jewish People?* (New York: Doubleday, 1968).

89. Fundamental Agreement between the Holy See and the State of Israel, signed Dec. 30, 1993, http://www.mfa.gov.il/MFA/MFAArchive/1990_1999/1993/12/Fundamental+Agreement+-+Israel-Holy+See.htm.

90. Ernest Renan, *The Life of Jesus* (London: Trubner and Co., 1876), 282.

91. St. Augustine, Epistle 82.

92. St. Augustine, Against Faustus, XII.11, http://www.logoslibrary.org/augustine/faustus/1211.html.

93. Augustine, Reply to Faustus the Manichaen, XII.11, http://www.ccel.org/ccel/schaff/npnf104.iv.ix.xiv.html.

94. Chrysostom, Homilies against the Jews, http://holywar.org/txt/chrysostom.html.

95. *Summa Theologica*, part 3, question 68.

96. Martin Luther, *On the Jews and Their Lies,* http://www.humanitas-international.org/showcase/chronography/documents/luther-jews.htm.

97. Eliezer Berkovits, *Faith After the Holocaust* (New York: KTAV Publishing, 1973), 17.

98. John Cornwell, *Hitler's Pope* (New York: Penguin, 1999), 209.

99. Daniel Goldhagen, "Did the Pope Steal Holocaust Children?" *Sunday Times.* January 9, 2005. http://www.timesonline.co.uk/tol/news/article409960.ece.

100. Ibid.

101. Matthew 27:46 NIV.

102. Mark 15:16–20 NIV.

103. Luke 23:35 NIV.

104. John 3:16 NIV.

105. Ibid. 18:6, 19:38–42 NIV.

106. Ibid. 19:11 NIV.

107. Mark 16:1–4 NIV.

108. Matthew 28:1 NIV.

109. John 20:1 NIV.

110. Wilhem Schneemelcher, ed. *New Testament Apocrypha, Volume One: Gospels and Related Writings* (Louisville, KY: Westminster John Knox Press, 2003), 223.

111. Acts 2:36 NIV.

112. Ibid. 5:30 NIV.

113. Ibid. 3:13 NIV (emphasis added).

114. Matthew 26:31–34 NIV.

115. Ibid. 26:70 NIV.

116. Ibid. 26:73–74 NIV.

117. Luke 13:31 NIV.

118. Augustine, Homilies on the Gospel of John; Homilies on the First Epistle of John; Soliloquies XI:12.

119. Quoted in Hyam Maccoby, *Judas Iscariot and the Myth of Jewish Evil* (New York: Free Press, 1992), 122.

120. Luke 22:3 NIV.

121. John 13:27 NIV.

122. Ibid. 13:2 NIV.

123. Ibid. 12:3–6 NIV.

124. Maccoby, *Judas Iscariot and the Myth of Jewish Evil*, 63.

125. Ibid.

126. John 18:1–5 NIV.

127. Raymond Brown, *The Death of the Messiah* (New York: Doubleday, 1999), 1395.

128. Maccoby, *Judas Iscariot and the Myth of Jewish Evil*, 88.

129. Ibid.

130. 2 Samuel 17:1–3 NIV.

131. Mark 14:43–45 NIV.

132. 2 Samuel 17:23 NIV.

133. Matthew 27:3, 5 NIV.

134. Maccoby, *Judas Iscariot and the Myth of Jewish Evil*, 43.

135. Acts 1:15–20 NIV.

136. Numbers 5:11–31 NIV.

137. Maccoby, *Judas Iscariot and the Myth of Jewish Evil*, 83.

138. Matthew 27:22–25 NIV.

139. Ibid. 21:8–9 NIV.

140. Philo, *The Works of Philo Judaeus, the Contemporary of Josephus*, vol. 4, translated by C.D. Yonge (London: H.G. Bohn, 1855), 165.

141. Josephus, *Jewish Antiquities*, 783.

142. Cornelius Tacitus, *Annals* 15:44.

143. Gregory Baum, *The Jews and the Gospel* (Westminster, MD: Newman Press, 1961), 72.

144. Luke 13:1–3 NIV.

145. Mark 15:6–15, Matthew 27:15–26, Luke 23:18–19, John 18:40 NIV.

146. Mark 15:6–11 NIV.

147. Philo, *Against Flaccus*, 81–84, quoted in John Dominic Crossan, *Jesus: A Revolutionary Biography* (New York: HarperCollins, 1995), 141.
148. Hyam Maccoby, "Jesus and Barabbas," *New Testament Studies* 16 (1968): 55–60.
149. Mark 15:42–46 NIV.
150. Matthew 27:57–59 NIV.
151. Sanhedrin 11b.
152. Ibid. 32b.
153. John Dominic Crossan, *Who Killed Jesus?* (New York: HarperCollins, 1995), 117.
154. Mark 3:6 NIV; Matthew 12:14 NIV.
155. Maccoby, *The Mythmaker*, 33–34.
156. Numbers 24:17 NIV.
157. Jerusalem Talmud, Ta'anit 4:8.
158. Ibid.
159. *Mishneh Torah, Hilchot Melachim* 11:1–4.
160. http://www.chabad.org/library/moshiach/article_cdo/aid/101744/jewish/NIVaws-Concerning-Kings-and-the-Messiah.htm.
161. Rabbi Shmuel Boteach, *The Wolf Shall Lie with the Lamb: The Messiah in Hasidic Thought* (Jason Aronson, 1993).
162. Deuteronomy 14:1 NIV.
163. Ezekiel 9:9–10 NIV.
164. Jeremiah 7:14–15 NIV.
165. Gittin 56a–b.
166. Ezekiel 40:2–4 NIV.
167. John 15:10 NIV.
168. Matthew 15:10–11 NIV.
169. Leviticus 19:16 NIV.
170. Proverbs 12:18 NIV.
171. Psalms 19:14 NIV.
172. Proverbs 16:23 NIV.
173. Ibid. 22:11 NIV.
174. Ibid. 23:15–16 NIV.
175. Acts 22:3–6 NIV.
176. Maccoby, *The Mythmaker*, 71.
177. 1 Corinthians 15:55 NIV.
178. Deuteronomy 21:23.
179. Galatians 3:13 NIV.
180. Ibid. 3:25 NIV.

181. Romans 7:1–6 NIV.
182. Acts 22:27 NIV.
183. Ibid. 26:9–12 NIV.
184. Romans 11:1 NIV.
185. Maccoby, *The Mythmaker*, 96.
186. Ibid., 60.
187. Galatians 1:13–14 NIV.
188. Matthew 15:24 NIV.
189. Acts 15:1–5 NIV.
190. 1 Thessalonians 2:14–16 NIV.
191. 1 Corinthians 9:23 NIV.
192. Ibid. 9:19–22 NIV.
193. Galatians 3:14 NIV.
194. Acts 21:20–22 NIV.
195. Ibid. 23–25 NIV.
196. Galatians 2:11–14 NIV.
197. Acts 10:10–15 NIV.
198. Phillip Schaff, *History of the Christian Church*, vol. 2 (New York: Scribner, 1867), 380.
199. Mark 12:17.
200. Matthew 23:33–36 NIV.
201. John 8:44 NIV.
202. Ibid. 8:19 NIV.
203. Ibid. 8:21 NIV.
204. Matthew 10: 5–6 NIV.
205. Matthew 15:24–26 NIV.
206. Michael L. Brown, *Answering Jewish Objections to Jesus,* vol. 1 (Grand Rapids, MI: Baker Books, 2000), 121.
207. Luke 6:27 NIV.
208. Luke 22:35–38 NIV.
209. Matthew 10:34–36 NIV.
210. Exodus 14:15 NIV.
211. *Mishneh Torah, Hilchot Melachim* 11:4.
212. Deuteronomy 4:15–16 NIV.
213. 1 Samuel 15:29 NIV.
214. Exodus 20:3–4 NIV.
215. Matthew 1:18 NIV.
216. Ibid. 1:20–23 NIV.
217. Isaiah 7:14, Judaica Press (emphasis added).

218. Proverbs 30:19 NIV.

219. Deuteronomy 6:4 NIV.

220. John 14:6 NIV.

221. Ibid. 20:21–23 NIV.

222. Psalms 145:18 NIV.

223. Exodus 20:3 NIV.

224. John 3:16 NIV.

225. St. Augustine, *On Concupiscence*, book 1, chap. 27.

226. Titus 3:4–7 NIV.

227. Deuteronomy 24:16 NIV.

228. Ezekiel 18:17 NIV.

229. Ibid. 18:19–20 NIV

230. Leviticus 4:2 NIV.

231. Ibid. 4:13–14 NIV.

232. Ibid. 4:22–23 NIV.

233. Ibid. 4:27–28 NIV.

234. Jonah 3:4 NIV.

235. Ibid. 3:8–9 NIV.

236. Ibid. 3:10 NIV.

237. Deuteronomy 12:31 NIV.

238. Ezekial 16:20–21 NIV.

239. Leviticus 17:11 NIV.

240. Ezekiel 40:38–39 NIV.

241. Ibid. 43:19–27 NIV.

242. Numbers 16:47 NIV.

243. Amos 5:21–22 NIV.

244. Jeremiah 7:22–23 NIV.

245. Numbers 5:7 NIV.

246. 2 Chronicles 7:14 NIV.

247. Psalms 40:6 NIV.

248. Leviticus 5:7 NIV.

249. Ibid. 5:11 NIV.

250. Hosea 14:2 NIV.

251. Proverbs 21:3 NIV.

252. Isaiah 11:1–2 NIV.

253. Jeremiah 23:5 NIV.

254. Charles G. Herbermann, *The Catholic Encyclopedia: An International Work of Reference on the Constituton, Doctrine, Discipline, and History of the*

Catholic Church, vol. 15 (New York: The Universal Knowledge Foundation Inc., 1912), 464E.

255. Matthew 1:1–6 NIV (emphasis added).

256. Ibid. 1:16 NIV.

257. Luke 3:23–31 NIV (emphasis added).

258. Herbermann, *The Catholic Encyclopedia*, 464E.

259. 1 Chronicles 22:9–10 NIV (emphasis added).

260. Matthew 1:17 NIV.

261. The four kings Matthew skips are listed in the otherwise identical list of Judean kings in 1 Chronicles 3:10–16.

262. Jeremiah 27:20 NIV.

263. Ibid. 22:30 NIV.

264. Malachi 4:5 NIV.

265. John 1:21 NIV.

266. Isaiah 11:6–9 NIV.

267. Jeremiah 31:34 NIV.

268. Isaiah 2:4 NIV.

269. Zechariah 9:10 NIV.

270. Ezekiel 39:9 NIV.

271. Psalms 72:7–9 NIV.

272. Zachariah 14:16 NIV.

273. Ibid. 13:2 NIV.

274. Ezekiel 37:26–27 NIV.

275. Isaiah 25:8 NIV.

276. Ibid. 26:19 NIV.

277. Ezekiel 37:12 NIV.

278. Ibid. 36:29 NIV.

279. Ibid. 47:12 NIV.

280. Ibid. 37:21 NIV.

281. Zechariah 8:23 NIV.

282. Isaiah 60:10 NIV.

283. Matthew 24:34 NIV.

284. Mark 1:15 NIV.

285. Luke 21:29–31 NIV.

286. James 5:8–10 NIV.

287. Matthew 26:64 NIV.

288. Revelations 22:7.

289. Galatians 3:25 NIV.

290. Genesis 17:7 NIV.

291. 2 Samuel 23:5 NIV.

292. 1 Chronicles 16:17 NIV.

293. Deuteronomy 29:29 NIV.

294. Matthew 5:18–19 NIV.

295. Brown, *Answering Jewish Objections to Jesus*, 28.

296. Ibid., 29–30.

297. Ibid., 117.

298. Augustine of Hippo, *Enchiridion on Faith, Hope, and Love* XXXI:118.

299. Brown, *Answering Jewish Objections to Jesus*, 30.

300. Ibid., 32.

301. Ibid., 33.

302. Ibid., 196.

303. Ibid., 30.

304. Ibid., 33.

305. *Ethics of the Fathers* 1:3.

306. Deuteronomy 30:15 NIV.

307. Ibid. 30:19 NIV.

308. Gittin 61a.

309. Tosefta Bava Metzia 2:11.

310. Tosefta Bava Kamma 10:8.

311. Tosefta Sanhedrin 13:1.

312. Jerusalem Talmud, Peah 1:1.

313. Midrash Sifra, Acharei Mot 9:13.

314. John 3:36 NIV.

315. Ibid. 15:6 NIV.

316. Mark 16:16 NIV.

317. Exodus Rabbah 2:2.

318. *Ethics of the Fathers* 4:3.

319. http://www.time.com/time/specials/2007/article/0,28804,1720049_1720050_1721663,00.html#ixzz14tzst3x9.

320. Joshua Shenk, *Lincoln's Melancholy: How Depression Challenged a President and Fueled His Greatness* (New York: Mariner, 2006), 50–51.

321. Matthew 27:46 NIV.

322. Ibid. 10:34 NIV.

323. Genesis 18:25 NIV.

324. Philippians 3:8–9 NIV.

325. Matthew 5:18–19 NIV.

326. Hyun Sik Kim, "Consequences of Parental Divorce for Child Development," *American Sociological Review* 76 (June 2011), http://www.asanet.org/images/journals/docs/pdf/asr/Jun11ASRFeature.pdf.

327. Sanhedrin 43a.

328. Ibid.

329. Robert H. Stein, *Jesus the Messiah: A Survey of the Life of Christ* (Downers Grove, IL: InterVarsity Press, 1996), 76.

330. Josephus, *Wars of the Jews*, book VI, V:3.

331. Sotah 47a. Translation from *Talmud Bavli: Tractate Sotah*, vol. 2 (New York: Mesorah, 2000), Sotah 47a4.

332. Menachem HaMeiri, *Beit Habechirah*, Sotah 47a.

333. Marcus Jastrow, *A Dictionary of the Targumim, the Talmud Babli and Yerushalmi, and the Midrashic Literature* (New York: G. P. Putnam's Sons, 1903), 930.

334. Maimonides, *Letter to Yemen*.